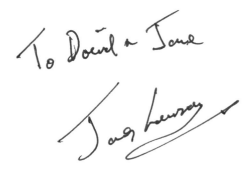

EVACUATE!

James Lawson

D1612455

ATHENA PRESS
LONDON

EVACUATE!
Copyright © James Lawson 2010

All Rights Reserved

ISBN 978 1 84748 776 6

First published 2010 by
ATHENA PRESS
Queen's House, 2 Holly Road
Twickenham TW1 4EG
United Kingdom

Printed for Athena Press

EVACUATE!

About this Book

This is the true story of how, at the end of 1978 and early 1979, some 1,300 expatriates and their families, working in the oilfields of southern Iran, were safely evacuated from the country at the time of the Iranian Revolution, when the Shah of Iran was deposed and Ayatollah Khomeini seized power. All escaped safely, except one: my dear friend and colleague, Paul Grimm, of Texaco. This short book is dedicated to his memory and that of his charming wife, Burdeen. It is also dedicated, with thanks, to the management, pilots and cabin staff of Gulf Air, whose professionalism, skill and courage in coming into Abadan Airport and rescuing us was an outstanding feat. To all of us evacuated by Gulf Air, it will always remain the best airline in the world.

Author's Note

It may seem strange to some that the events covered by this short book relate to just over thirty years ago – at the time of the Iranian Revolution. However, I did wish to record them, as I believe that what happened then, in Iran, and what is still occurring now, are all relevant as an insight into the Iranian people's 'psyche'; the way they see themselves and the way they are viewed by the Western world. The recent martyrdom in 2009 of Neda Agha-Soltan, the twenty-six-year-old student shot dead during the protests after the summer's disputed elections, has become a symbol of the divide at the heart of Iran. The younger, educated, intellectual Iranians seek peaceful coexistence with the West, freedom of speech, true democracy, human rights and a more libertarian lifestyle, while the rulers and the mullahs still try to impose a harsh, unjust and authoritarian regime. We need to do all in our power to help these young people attain their goals. One must also remember the increasing threat of such an unstable and anti-West regime becoming a nuclear power in the very near future (if it is not that already). This needs the most careful of handling and an increase in dialogue, rather than the threat of a pre-emptive 'strike' by either America or Israel. As one has seen from the (probably) unjustified war in Iraq, and the failures so far in Afghanistan, with ever-increasing NATO Forces casualties, these indicate quite forcibly that war is not an option for the future.

Prologue

It would perhaps be helpful, by way of introduction, to explain, briefly, my background and how it was that I ended up being in Iran at the time of the Revolution in the first place – and I blame that on my three daughters, who were being educated at boarding school in England. Even in those days, three sets of boarding school fees three times a year were pretty impossible on a UK salary (even a good one), particularly after the taxation levels then prevalent.

Born in Dundee in 1936, I lived through the Second World War as a child, remembering our iron garden wall railings being cut down to go towards the war effort; my father, commanding the local unit of the Home Guard, going out every time the air raid sirens went off; the blackout, our windows taped against bomb blasts, and my duties being to empty and refill the bottles of water stored with some rations in the makeshift air raid shelter built under our stairs. I also remember carrying my gas mask at all times on my way to school at the Harris Academy, and helping to make sure that no light escaped from our curtains at night, lest we incurred the wrath of the local ARP warden.

While Dundee suffered very little compared to other cities, the Tay Rail Bridge, not so far away from us, was a major target, and several attempts were made by the German Luftwaffe to bomb it – resulting in one house 200 yards away from us being bombed and the occupants killed.

At the age of eight I was sent away to boarding school in

7

Pitlochry, and then on to Merchiston Castle School in Edinburgh, which I enjoyed hugely, both educationally and in terms of sport and the Army Cadet Force. We were a 'Gunner' (Royal Artillery) ACF which is why, following my call-up papers to do my national service at the age of eighteen, I ended up doing my duty in the 32nd Medium Regiment, following being commissioned as an officer. Suez then intervened, which meant that I stayed on for an extra year. This included the ultimately fruitless exercise of going out towards Egypt and then coming back again, after the Americans forbade Anthony Eden to go in and save the Suez Canal. Had we been allowed to proceed, the Middle East, in my view, would not be in the turmoil it is now.

Coming out of the army in 1957 I was really given no other choice by my father but to study law and become the third generation of lawyers in our family – my grandfather, Hubert, having founded our family law firm in the late 1800s. As I had served in the armed forces, I was allowed a 'fast track' route to qualify in three years, instead of five, by doing my apprenticeship in a law firm and at the same time attending lectures at Queens College, Dundee – then part of St Andrews University – and qualified as a solicitor in 1960, joining my father in the family law firm.

After the first few years I became restless, as I yearned to go into international commercial law and our practice was very much domestic; with property, wills, executory work and the like. My father was the eldest of five, and as there was only room for him in the family law firm all the other four (as was common in those days) ended up abroad in Ceylon, India, Canada and Australia, although one returned to Leicester as a doctor; I think that this is where my 'wanderlust' came from.

So, to my father's horror (although we were later

reconciled), I left Dundee and went south to England, determined to go into the wider world, taking with me my wife and three young daughters.

While I was studying to become qualified in England (the Scots having a separate legal system) I saw an advertisement for a post as legal counsel to the London office of a very large American engineering and construction company called Bechtel. So I applied for the post, and to my astonishment landed the job.

There then followed the most exciting years of my life (until Iran!).

Bechtel

Bechtel was the most extraordinary company for which to work. Founded in the USA in 1898 by Warren Bechtel, it started life with one steam shovel and Irish immigrant labour building railroads across America. On reaching San Francisco, that became the headquarters of what had become, when I joined it, the largest firm of construction engineers in the world.

The company was then, and still is to this day, privately owned and was divided into several major divisions. These included nuclear, refineries and chemicals, pipelines, mining and metals, building construction etc.; there were no areas of major projects where Bechtel did not have experience and expertise.

The London offices were, when I started there, in Portman Square just off Oxford Street and I was immediately impressed, not only by the very warm welcome I received on my first day, but also by the sheer professionalism and dedication of the staff employed there. Many of the senior staff were Americans, and there were some great characters among them: Bill Hannah, a huge, larger-than-life Vice President of Construction; Myrle Perkins of Business Development; and Chuck Lester of Pipelines, just to name but a few. On the UK side, Peter Sharp in accounting and Dudley Pugh in contracts, people with whom I was to work closely, quickly became good friends and showed this very obvious 'greenhorn' the ropes.

The work I had to undertake was so hugely different

from that which I had left in Scotland, but so amazingly varied and enthralling. For example, at the time I joined Bechtel, the UK sector of the North Sea was beginning to prove that there were significant reservoirs of oil and gas offshore, and we worked very hard on that. Bechtel won a contract, which I helped to negotiate, for a semi-submersible production platform for the Argyll Field, and we were very proud to beat BP to the punch for the first commercial oil ashore ahead of Forties.

The advert for a legal counsel to which I had responded had mentioned 'some international travel', and that turned out to be a masterpiece of understatement. Paris was a frequent point of call as Bechtel had no in-house lawyer there, and their Paris office was developing major contracts in Algeria (also French-speaking) with Sonatrach, the Algerian State Oil Company. Maurice Cori, who ran the Paris office, was a superb gourmet, who insisted that lunch was always a serious affair of at least two hours and developed my love of oysters, frogs' legs and snails.

Next came Mauretania, where we negotiated contracts for a major mining plant. The Bechtel 'ethos' was very rigid and well structured. I generally worked in a team comprising a divisional vice-president, the project manager to be, if we got the contract, and me as the legal counsel. Bechtel had a voluminous set of 'directives' which laid down strict parameters of the conditions of the contract terms we could accept and the limitation on liabilities encompassed therein, and it was a cardinal rule that no Bechtel vice-president could sign any form of contract unless the final pre-signature draft had been signed and stamped by one of Bechtel's legal counsel as being 'approved as to form and content'. So the 'team of three' usually formed a very strong and powerful relationship. It was always my endeavour to really try to understand and grasp the technology involved, and had I had my time again, I would have qualified with a degree in engineering and law.

Following Mauretania came Libya, where Bechtel had a considerable presence and an office in Tripoli, but again no in-house lawyer. Hence, when contract problems and disputes arose, I was frequently asked for. At the start, Libya was ruled by King Idris (with whom Bechtel had a strong and warm relationship), and Tripoli was a pleasure to visit, with good hotels, excellent food, a relaxed lifestyle and entertainment from the Americans at the Whelus base further along the coast. I enjoyed my visits there and the great hospitality of British Caledonian Airways, with their tartan-clad stewardesses, who were great fun and stayed at the same hotel. After the revolution, Libya, under Ghadaffi, was a different kettle of fish – very different, and no alcohol! I used to scrounge a few miniatures from the flight and sneak them into my briefcase – enough to give me one miniature each night.

I was in the London office one day when a telex came in from Tripoli that there had been a major fire and explosion in a gas re-injection plant that Bechtel were building, and they urgently needed a lawyer out there and an insurance expert. As all Bechtel's insurance was handled by Willis Faber, the insurance brokers in London, I got hold of my good friend Ninian Hawkin and we set off for Tripoli. On arrival, we were briefed by the Tripoli manager, who told us that Ghadaffi's troops had sealed off the site and that the situation was pretty serious. An old converted Lancaster bomber was to fly us down towards the border with Chad, and we arrived there to start our investigations. The Project Manager met us, and we had military beside us all the time as we went to examine the damage and question staff. It rapidly became obvious what the cause of the fire was. Some Libyan subcontractors had been painting the newly constructed cooling towers with a highly flammable paint. The area was a 'hot' zone, which meant that no fire or matches or cigarettes would be permitted in the zone – but somehow the subcontractors had filled a jerrycan with sand and petrol and lit it, in the traditional way, to brew up tea at the lunch break... and the whole thing had gone up in flames. As Ninian and I were reaching our conclusion, the army arrested us and took us off to a searing hot tin hut where we were kept for hours with two Libyan soldiers pointing old .303 Lee Enfield rifles at us.

After an age, we were told we were being taken to jail in Agedabia and charged with 'exploiting the brave Libyan people and falsely blaming them for the fire that had been caused by Americans'. The Project Manager managed to get us a crate of beer (which was allowed on site), and we were bundled into a Land Rover with a driver and three guards. Ninian and I offered them a beer, and as they were not used to alcohol the effect on them was quite dramatic. When they had to stop to relieve themselves, they handed us their rifles to look after while they went for a pee!

Conditions in Agedabia jail were pretty basic, but fortunately Ninian had served in Libya during the war and knew some Arabic, and we detected a certain sympathy to our plight. We were not handcuffed and were given a reasonably clean but stiflingly hot cell, which we shared and mused on our plight and our future. Word of our arrest had, obviously, been conveyed by the Project Manager to the manager of the Tripoli office and by this time I had an assistant lawyer, an Australian called David James, and he was flown down to Agedabia along with the Bechtel Project Manager and the British Consul to try to negotiate our release. During our questioning we were asked to sign a document stating that the cause of the fire and explosion had been negligence on Bechtel's part and that it had been 'American imperialist exploitation of the brave Libyan people' – a document that both Ninian and I declined to sign.

As I understand it, Bechtel kept a reasonably substantial supply of American dollars under the floorboards in the Tripoli office to 'ease its way through officialdom' in getting necessary permits, visas etc., and while neither Ninian nor I were present, we understand that a Libyan Bechtel employee secured our release against a pretty substantial but undisclosed donation to the Chief of Police's favourite charity!

We were then flown from Agedabia to Tripoli, where we had large expulsion orders stamped on our passports, and were put on a British Caledonian plane back to London; the stewardesses were wonderful, and the minute the plane was taxiing for take-off we had glasses of champagne in our hands, followed by a superb meal. Needless to say, I never went back to Libya again, but Bechtel completed the job and the insurers paid up. Little did I know at that time that I would later have a similar experience in Kuwait.

The next major contract was in Zambia where, along with the Bechtel Vice-President of Refineries and Pipelines and the Project Manager, we negotiated a contract with the Zambian Ministry of Development for the construction of a refinery at Ndola and a lengthy pipeline from Dar es Salaam on the coast to the refinery site. That meant frequent visits to Zambia, and in those days we stopped at Entebbe in Uganda to refuel, and went inside the airport and had breakfast – a very sensible use of the time, and fortunately before Idi Amin had become so dangerous.

The pipeline construction contract was negotiated with the Italian company Snamprogetti, based in Milan, and that resulted in many trips there and from there on to Ndola in Zambia. We were always very well looked after by the Italians and I remember three-hour lunches at San Donato Milanese, followed by very late dinners in Milan itself – not good for the figure!

I recall that we were in Zambia with the Italians and the Zambian government officials, trying to finalise Snamprogetti's contract terms; we had started on a Monday and negotiations were very tough, and by Thursday we had made little progress, so on the Friday morning I told the Italians that, as we had a long way to go, I had cancelled their Friday evening flights back to Milan, and that we would work through the weekend until we had reached an agreement. Surprisingly, as the morning and early afternoon progressed, points of disagreement seemed to be overcome, with the Italians more and more accepting of the terms – so much so that by about 4.30 p.m. we had reached an agreement and had an initialled final draft contract. The Snamprogetti team immediately dashed off to the airport in a desperate attempt to catch the evening flight to Milan. By that time, first class was full and they had to book economy. They were somewhat surprised to see me at the first-class check-in desk (Bechtel always flew us 'in the front', as they thought it good for 'business development'). Some time after take-off, two or three of the Italians came to the first-class cabin to enquire how I had got a first-class seat, and I said to them, 'Gentlemen, I told you this morning that I had cancelled your flights but I did not say that I had cancelled mine!'

By this time, I was doing so much travelling that it began to take its toll on my marriage; so often I promised to be there for one of my three daughters' birthdays, sports day, play or other event and so many times I had to let them down as 'the job came first' and I was away, yet again, in foreign parts. By this time we had bought a house in Henley-on-Thames and I was commuting daily to Bechtel's new offices in Hammersmith or, frequently, Heathrow Airport.

The next major project was a Liquefied Natural Gas project for BP on Das Island in the Middle East. So many of the Bechtel staff on the project were based in Bechtel's head office in San Francisco that it was decided that, as the nominated Bechtel Attorney, I should move there on a temporary basis while the contract was negotiated and finalised. I went out on single status, and Bechtel agreed to fly me back once a month to see my wife and children for a long weekend. We usually flew TWA, and these trips were economy, not first class; however my TWA 'fly over lady', who got to know me quite well, was able to offer me a fourteen-to-twenty-one-day special-offer excursion that would enable me to fly over twice a month for the price of one full fare economy ticket – which Bechtel paid for. It was somewhat weird, as I was issued with two round-trip tickets and I flew out on the outward half of the first ticket and back on the return half of the second ticket and then vice versa for the second voyage, i.e. out on the first half of the second ticket and back on the second half of the first ticket!

My boss was a most wonderful man, Bill Slusser, the worldwide President of Legal Services from whom I got enormous support throughout my time with Bechtel. I remember bumping into him in the elevator at Beale Street in San Francisco with his lunch guest and he introduced me warmly as 'one of his more colourful attorneys' – whatever that meant! The Vice-President in charge of Business Development for the Das Island project was, again, a person whom I came to like and respect greatly, Carl Minden, and we remained friends long after I left and he had retired. Sadly Carl died in 2001.

The negotiations of the contract with BP were enormously complex, and strained whatever drafting talents I had to the limit. It was a multi-currency contract with a strong Japanese presence, as they were to fund the construction of the Cryogenic Units needed on Das Island and on the ships transporting the LNG from Das Island to Japan – these ships being literally floating time bombs if ever they were to be attacked or be in a collision.

We had to make frequent trips to London to negotiate with BP, but also to Tokyo to negotiate and finalise the contract with the Japanese trading house and manufacturing company. Carl Minden was a deep thinker on negotiating strategy and used to come to my room after our day's work was over, pace the hotel room and use me as a sounding board as to how we were to go about resolving seemingly impossible differences of opinion relative to realistic contract and financial terms – but we got there!

When I moved to San Francisco, Bechtel had rented me a serviced bachelor apartment near the office, but the evenings were lonely until I got to know people. One of the attorneys on the twenty-second floor, Ron Hartsough, who was a bachelor with a beautiful house in Piedmont, suggested I room with him. He has remained a close and loyal friend to this day. We had some fantastic barbecues and parties, which cushioned the loneliness of being out there on single status.

Other contracts were on the go at the same time, including a plant for Iron Ore of Canada and Hydro

Quebec, which was an enormous power generation facility, so I saw a good deal of Eastern Canada as well. Very sadly, all of the Bechtel senior project team were killed in an air crash in a chartered aircraft near Churchill Falls and I felt so lucky, as I might well have been on that plane.

In the early 1970s Bechtel was awarded the management of a huge project in France to construct the first post-war new steel-making complex, which was to be built at Fos-sur-Mer, near Marseille. As I understand it, the Bechtel President, Steve Bechtel Snr, was at the signing ceremony with the French President when he was told that the whole project had to be done in French, on the basis of national pride. Steve had replied that, as a multinational company, if the President wanted it done in French, Bechtel would, of course, comply. Immediately afterwards the Vice-President of Personnel was called to find out 'who the hell in our organisation speaks French?'

Well, I have to admit that in my CV, as part of my application to join Bechtel some years before, I had somewhat overstated my linguistic skills; I was comfortably ensconced in my super office overlooking San Francisco Bay when Bill Slusser walked in and said, 'James, we have just appointed you as Contracts Manager for the French Steel Project – you leave for Metz [on the Franco–German border, where the project started] the day after tomorrow!'

When I arrived in Metz, I got a pretty frosty reception from the French Engineering Group (GEA), the contracts section of whom were all working in the requisitioned Hôtel de Ville, which literally still had the walls pockmarked with bullet holes from the Second World War. The staff were all rushing about jabbering in very fast French and I was shown to a desk in a corner with a telephone and two wire baskets – 'out' and 'in' trays. I sat there for a while

– the rest of the day, in fact – and nothing came into my in tray, so there was nothing to go out, and my telephone never rang. All the contract project staff had been put up at the local Novotel, and when I went into the bar in the evening I was studiously ignored, the French at one end and me at the other.

I stuck the same treatment for one more day – the French were all rushing about muttering about *appel d'offres*, and I didn't even know that was the French for a bid invitation! However, the following morning I came into the office, shut the door and told them that I was the boss and in charge and that if they were not prepared to cooperate, I would insist that I saw every document that came into the office and see and approve everything that went out of it. This was met by a chorus of protest, saying that the tendering process for contracts was already way behind schedule, that they did not need American *parapluie* (umbrella) management and I would only make delays worse. However, I stuck to my guns, and with a vengeance my in basket was loaded and the telephone started to ring. By that evening at the Novotel, the French had got to know that I was not American but Scottish. It was the sixtieth birthday of one of the French contract staff and he, Michel Mazères, came to my end of the bar and invited me to join them. That really broke the ice and the following morning, in the office, everyone came to shake my hand – as they did every day I was on the project – and we began to make real progress.

After a month or so in Metz, I had to go down to site to meet the American Project Manager, Bill Mellon, to sort out the logistics of my group moving from Metz to Fos-sur-Mer, and I had somebody out renting every available house in the surrounding area to cope with the influx of Bechtel staff once construction got underway. On the second trip down there, we chartered a private plane to take most of the project team down for a site visit, and while I was sorting out the insurance cover for the flight with Bechtel Legal and Insurance in San Francisco, remembering the Churchill Falls tragedy in Canada, in a telex I queried the wisdom of putting all the project team in one aircraft. Back came the terse reply, 'What's so special about you?'

My wife and three daughters were due to join me once a house had been allocated to us, and we ended up in a charming newbuild in a lovely little village called Grans, not far from Salon-de-Provence, and I drove my little Peugeot to site and back every day. The Bechtel furniture removers had come into our house in Henley-on-Thames, packed everything up and delivered it to 'Villa Martini' as the house was called. The children, then aged about five, seven and nine, went straight away to the local school in Grans, not speaking a word of French, and found the teachers spoke very little English; however, such was the total immersion that after about three months we had to be sure to speak English at home so they did not forget their mother tongue. I remember their absolute horror when they discovered that the toilets were Asian 'stand-up' jobs!

The contract for the construction of this huge steel plant was very complex and involved many nationalities doing various bits of the plant under governmental funding from the respective countries involved – which included France, the UK, Russia, America and Japan. So, again, it meant more time away from home and put further strain on my marriage. I also became seriously ill with what was ultimately diagnosed as a diverticular tumour and was rushed back to the UK for emergency surgery; the French medical diagnosis had been that I had picked up a urinary infection from too many visits to the *femmes de la nuit* (ladies of the night!).

Bechtel were extraordinarily supportive and flew my family back to the UK while I convalesced, and then we returned to Grans and I got back on the project. My primary job was to get all the tenders out, the contracts awarded, and then pass them on to a team of American, English and French administrators, who took over from there. We had a real stand-off with the French contractors on site when Pete Behr, the Project Vice-President, declared that there would be no alcohol on site. Well, the French were accustomed to a proper one-hour lunch in the site canteen and to washing it down with half a litre or so of Côtes du Rhône; I leave you to guess who won!

I was urgently needed for another project in Russia and one in Japan, so I returned to San Francisco, to be followed some weeks later by my wife and children after the end of the school summer term. I had been found a house in Tiberon with a swimming pool, bought a beautiful Ford T-bird convertible and commuted over the Golden Gate Bridge to Beale Street every day. However, I was once again travelling long haul very frequently. I remember that, having flown eastwards, visiting London and various other countries such as Indonesia, and headed up to Japan, I used to have lunch with the Tokyo Office Manager on a Friday, and he took me for a three o'clock flight travelling east to San Francisco, crossing the date line and arriving in San Fran on early Friday morning – before I had left! My boss, Bill Slusser, usually took me to the very exclusive Bohemian Club for a second Friday lunch and frequently said, as we returned to the office, 'James, would you see my secretary, as she has some tickets and your flight schedule.' And as like or not, I was headed east again on the Sunday!

Sadly, I knew by this time that my wife had met someone else in Fos, while I was in hospital in the UK; and that Christmas my wife took the children back to England where the new man in her life was waiting for her. I am glad to say that we both worked hard at maintaining a good relationship – as did her new husband; we all wanted minimal stress for the children.

While I remained in San Francisco after the Christmas of 1973, I frequently headed east to the London office, then Saudi Arabia where we had two large top-secret projects, then on to Indonesia for a steel plant and an NGL facility; and as Indonesia was halfway round the world from San Francisco, inevitably it was into Tokyo again and then back to the USA.

On one of these trips we had two days in the London office and I was travelling with an American from Bechtel Insurance, Frank Keebough. One of my former colleagues, Dudley Pugh, had left Bechtel to join another colleague, Peter Sharp, who had also left earlier to set up his own firm, Penn Sharp, but they still had strong links with Bechtel, advising them on UK tax matters. Talking to Dudley on the phone, we suggested a night out together – but Dudley explained that there were a couple of girls in the office who had been working 'very hard and late' and that he was taking them for a night out. Well, we said that a bit of female company would be fine, and that we would come along too, teasing Dudley that, as a married man, it was up to us to look after the girls!

We ended up in the Barracuda Nightclub and were there dining and dancing until quite late the following morning. I was absolutely smitten by one of the girls and persuaded her to come and have dinner with me the following evening before we flew out. That dinner was a disaster. The young lady was very tired, disinterested in food and had the same view of me. However, I did know where she worked, and had her office phone number when I left! The next time round, when in London, I called her and suggested dinner but the answer was a firm 'no' – and it was the same the next two or even three times. I learnt later that she had put her hand over the mouthpiece of the phone to disguise her voice!

After three or four months Bechtel kindly transferred me back to London as their senior legal counsel there so that I could see more of my children, and I moved into a rented house in Maidenhead.

Basically, I was still responsible for the projects I had been working on from San Francisco, but I now worked out of the Hammersmith office in London and handled some new projects from there as well: refineries, pipelines, NGL plants, hotels for Intercontinental and major projects in Saudi Arabia. So it was back on the same old high-volume overseas travel again, and at one stage, I was flying round the world virtually once a month, as we had two major projects in Indonesia. The Tokyo office still needed me, and Bill Slusser and Barney Johnson, Head of Legal, succeeded later by my good friend John Mc Guinn, still liked me to call into the San Francisco office. Life as a bachelor was somewhat lonely.

I still tried calling the young lady, but the answer was still negative. However, one day she had to speak to me as I needed to make an appointment to see her boss, Peter, on Bechtel business for some tax advice; so we met again when I went to see Peter, and I feel that this might have been the beginning of a breakthrough – as I did get a smile and a handshake. The following day, I called again and did get to talk to her and I asked her out to dinner; but this was refused, although she did say cautiously that she might manage a lunch one day.

So we set a date and I researched a really top-class restaurant not far from her office, chose excellent wines and had my best suit on; it seemed to go well, as it was followed by a dinner date. A short while later, I had to go to the Bechtel office in Paris on business, and chose a Friday. I asked the lady along to make it a weekend; the answer was 'yes'… but she wanted her flatmate, Andrea, along as well!

Bovis

While I really loved my job with Bechtel, the travelling was really catching up with me. Before the days that DVTs were known to be a potential side effect of long-distance flying, I had had two pulmonary emboli, each two or three days after a long flight. Fortunately, on one occasion I was not far from Brompton Hospital in London, and was rushed there in an ambulance. The second time I collapsed in the street near Goodge Street station and ended up in University College Hospital intensive care unit. Having already had a post-operative thrombosis when I had my tumour removed, I was beginning to feel that I was using up too many lives!

Bovis were one of the largest construction companies in the UK and had several divisions from housing to major building projects. While I was at Bechtel I was frequently in touch with them as contractors for Bechtel for a large InterContinental Hotel, so I got to know their senior management quite well and was, effectively, headhunted to join them as Group Legal Advisor with a staff of eight other qualified lawyers and a total team of over one hundred.

Their head office was at Liscartan House in Sloane Street. It had a very relaxed and well-run atmosphere, and we worked in some considerable comfort. I was issued with a top of the range Jaguar XJ6, and when I arrived at the office from my rented house near Maidenhead, one of the chauffeurs would take the car away, wash it, valet it and fill up its two large tanks with petrol. Similarly, in my office, as we very frequently were having meetings with potential clients, every morning one of the waitresses would come in and make sure that my well-stocked bar had all that was needed and provided fresh lemon and ice. We usually arranged meetings with potential contract customers around 11 a.m., opened the bar at twelve and then took them upstairs to one of the best private dining rooms in London for an excellent lunch, washed down with Grand Cru Classé wines, followed by cheese and vintage port – or a brandy or two. Our chauffeurs were always on standby to take what was left of our guests back to their respective offices; the funny thing is that after one of these lunches, if you did telephone one of the guests on business thereafter, you were always put through!

The Chief Executive of Bovis was a most charming man, Neville Vincent, who had the most wonderful sense of humour and was a great raconteur at these lunches. Malcolm Paris, the Finance Director, and I worked very closely together, as I dealt with the commercial terms of all the major contracts we negotiated. There was some travel overseas involved as Bovis had a business in Paris and ambitions of doing major projects in the Middle East.

As part of our corporate hospitality we had two boxes at Ascot, which 'had to be used' for client entertainment at all race meetings – including Royal Ascot – so I had to go out to Moss Bros and buy a set of tails, a top hat and apply to Her Majesty's Representative for entry to the Royal Enclosure. A most super retired naval officer, Commander Derek Williams, organised all the hospitality at Ascot, and was always there to guide the wives of our clients through the vagaries and intricacies of the horse betting system.

On the domestic side, my romantic intentions were progressing favourably, with increasingly frequent visits to Teddington to the young lady's flat, which she shared with

Andrea – the chaperone on our first trip to Paris when I was still with Bechtel. I found the frequent trips from Teddington to Maidenhead late at night most inconvenient, and so started looking around at properties for sale in the Teddington area. As the children often stayed with me over a weekend, I needed a house big enough to cope with them, as well as my own domestic requirements.

There were some townhouses being built near the Thames that looked as if they might suit, and I thought that, as she might one day end up living there, I should ask my girlfriend's opinion by showing her the almost finished house. I remember saying to her, 'For example, is it a place and a house you would like to live in?' – to which I was given the very short answer, 'If you think I'm moving in with you – forget it!' So I knew that I had to progress matters with a little more patience and delicacy.

Gradually, my studious courtship bore fruit. I had bought the house in Teddington and asked the lady in question to marry me to which, to my delight, she had consented. I had been careful enough to have her get to know my three daughters reasonably well, and they gave the whole idea a somewhat cautious welcome. We fixed a date for our wedding on 2 March 1974 to be held in the London Scottish Chapel at St Columba's Scottish Presbyterian Church in Pont Street, London. Before proposing, we had flown to Dundee to seek my father's blessing (by now we were completely reconciled). He, in his shrewd judgement, sensed that I had made a very wise choice, and he and my stepmother, May, gave us their total support and approval.

In the midst of our wedding preparations and before the day itself, a major problem blew up at Bovis. We had an Executive Committee (of which I was a member) and we met once a month to agree and approve major decisions and the terms of bids for new contracts. As I have said earlier, Bovis had ambitions of opening up and bidding for construction projects in the Middle East. We were sitting at one of these meetings when the construction division, based in Harrow, advised us that they had bid for a civil engineering job in Kuwait for the Kuwaiti Ministry of Public Works, and due to the bidding deadline had had to go ahead and lodge the bid with the required 'Bid Bond' before there had been time to put it up for approval by the Executive Committee.

As we were discussing this item on the agenda, Neville Vincent's secretary came into the meeting and handed him a telex from Kuwait saying that Bovis had been awarded the contract and that, according to the terms of our tender, we were required in Kuwait the following Sunday with the not unsubstantial Performance Bond, and to sign the contract. Malcolm Paris and I, along with Bernard Heaphy, the Director at Harrow, were appointed urgently to look into this and the terms of the Bovis bid. With my experience of doing contracts overseas from my time with Bechtel, it was readily apparent that Bovis had completely underestimated the add-on costs of undertaking a contract in a foreign country, and that they would suffer heavy losses by doing this project in Kuwait.

Neville Vincent summoned me to his office and told me, very forcefully, that I had to go out to Kuwait immediately and negotiate Bovis's way out of this disastrous tender. George White, a senior manager from the Harrow office, was chosen to accompany me. He, by his own admission, had never been to the Middle East before – and this was less than two weeks before I was due to be married!

We duly arrived in Kuwait and checked into the Hilton Hotel and, as is typical, it was several days before the

Minster of Public Works agreed/condescended to meet us. We were ushered into his office, and I had been briefed to call him 'Your Excellency', as he was a member of the Kuwaiti royal family, a graduate of Oxford and spoke impeccable English, although wearing full Middle Eastern dress. I explained to him that I was very sorry but the bid Bovis had lodged with him had been an unauthorised tender, which had not been approved by the Executive Committee, and we wished to inform him that the bid was withdrawn. This did not go down well with the Minister of Public Works, who showed us that our bid was $2.1 million lower than the local Kuwaiti tendering contractor – which confirmed my worst fears that Bovis were really going to be incurring very heavy losses if we did the work! In those days you needed to add a multiplier of at least 2.5 to your UK bid if you were operating in the Middle East. As the meeting deteriorated I suggested that we could do the job at no profit – just at audited reimbursable cost – but this was forcefully declined. I repeated that the bid was a genuine error and that, if the Minister was not prepared to be reasonable, as we had no men and no equipment in Kuwait, Bovis would simply just not come. At that, the Sheikh jumped up, overturned the low coffee table and told us to get out, telling us that it was now going to cost him over $2 million more to get the project done.

George and I fled back to the Hilton and met in my room, wondering what to do next; we had to be careful what we said to London, as I knew it was likely that our phones were bugged and it was before the days of mobiles.

By this time, late evening, we were dying for a stiff drink and a meal, so George and I went up to the Hilton rooftop restaurant. Kuwait is of course 'dry' as far as alcohol is concerned, but I knew from previous visits to Kuwait, when with Bechtel, that if you asked in the restaurant for 'special tea' accompanied by a generous cash tip, you would be served a pot of 'tea' with two teacups – but it was, in fact, Johnny Walker Black Label – at a cost of £46 per bottle! We had no difficulty in polishing that off as we discussed our predicament. There was a popular tune going round at that time which started, 'It's impossible' – and it always seemed to be playing on the radio.

I arranged to meet George the following morning for breakfast and then try to arrange a further meeting with the Minister of Public Works, to see if he had calmed down a bit. However, as we got to the lobby on our way to break-fast, we were surrounded by lawyers in black robes waving papers at me, backed up by soldiers; as I suspected, I later discovered these were court writs, one against Bovis for $2.1 million and one against me personally for the same amount. I refused to accept them and they were stuffed into our room number pigeonholes, while George and I fled back to my room to discuss what to do.

We made a very careful call to London to say that we 'had a problem' and I also asked them to alert my fiancée that I might be a bit late back to the UK, and that she should go to the registrar's to collect our marriage lines, which I was supposed to deliver to Pont Street Church. My view, expressed to George, was that as things had turned so nasty and with writs flying around, it was time to get out. So we very carefully waited until midday prayers and then sneaked down to the lobby to leave. The mistake I made, I believe, was in paying our hotel bill before we left, as this must have been fed back to the authorities, as we were to learn shortly.

When we got to Kuwait Airport, I looked at the depar-tures board and the first plane going out was to Delhi – nothing to the UK for many hours. I said to my companion,

'Ever been to Delhi, George?' He shook his head and I told him I had been there and it was a great place; so I bought two tickets to Delhi and we went through immediately to the departure lounge, where I said that we had better wait in the toilets until the flight was called, in case we were being looked for and spotted. After about thirty minutes the tannoy started blaring, '*Arayah* [Mr] *Lawson, Arayah White!*' and we could hear soldiers in there, so we knew that the game was up.

We were taken back into Kuwait City and told we were under arrest as it was a criminal offence to attempt to leave Kuwait with a Government writ outstanding against you, and we were kept in custody for several hours, our passports confiscated. I had asked for the British Embassy to be informed and some time later the British Consul appeared and explained that the Ambassador was on leave, but that he would do his best for us, through diplomatic channels. We gave him Bernard Heaphy and Neville Vincent's contact details and the Foreign Office got to work. Rather than have us detained in jail, the Consul vouched for our good behaviour, so it was back to the Hilton (without our passports) under hotel arrest – this time in one room.

Meanwhile the date of my wedding in London was getting even closer, and there were serious doubts that we would be released in time for me to make it. The Consul had an idea that, as there was a British frigate on a goodwill visit to Kuwait, they would fly my fiancée out as a ship's officer and that I would be given a naval rating's uniform and go on-board where the captain would marry us!

We were aware from the Consul that there was some pretty furious activity with Bovis and the Foreign Office to try to secure our release. In the upshot a 'flash' telex was sent from the Foreign Office to the Kuwaiti Government, which included Neville Vincent's public apology to Kuwait for Bovis's behaviour in general and my conduct in particular; this was accepted by the Kuwaiti authorities. George and I were summoned back to the court and had large red expulsion orders stamped on our passports and, just a few days before my wedding, we were driven out to Kuwait Airport. Here they had held a British Airways VC10, on its way back from Kuala Lumpur, on the tarmac for three hours until we were bundled on-board. The captain greeted us, we were given first-class seats and that first glass of champagne as the plane took off was absolutely wonderful – although I don't think the other passengers were all that chuffed at the three-hour delay!

Bernard Heaphy himself came to the airport to meet us on the Saturday, and made sure that my darling fiancée was there also – it was a great reunion. I will always thank and remember Bernard for that kind gesture, and I am glad to say that we are still in touch to this day. Despite what had happened in Kuwait, Bovis did end up doing the contract there, on a cost reimbursable basis.

Many of my family, my father included, came down for our wedding a few days later at Pont Street, and at long last Ginny (as that is her name!) and I were married – with Andrea as matron of honour! We had a wonderful wedding brunch at a super French restaurant and George, one of the Bovis chauffeurs, told Ginny that we were going to Brighton – and to start with he did head off down the M3, but then went into Heathrow the 'back' way and we flew off to Paris to start our honeymoon. We stayed for one night at the Hôtel Régina with a superb dinner at the Tastevin restaurant, with the best duck à l'orange and soufflé Grand Marnier one could ever imagine. We then had a fantastic week in Morocco. On our return, we had a couple of days before we took the children off skiing to Isola 2000 in France, where the girls had skied before. They were very excited and the morning after we had arrived they rushed in from the adjoining bedroom and leapt into our bed – very surprised that 'stepma' didn't wear a nightie!

On the business and industrial front in the mid-1970s things got very tough, with a great deal of industrial unrest, which culminated in the miners' strike. The Bovis trading situation suffered severely, as did many other companies; we had been in discussions for some time with regard to a takeover or merger with P&O, the shipping conglomerate, as they also had a property division in trouble and Frank Sanderson, our racehorse-owning chairman, was secretly having discussions with Lord Inchcape, Chairman of P&O. Worst of all, it appeared that he had not informed his Chief Executive, Neville Vincent, what he was up to.

The money markets got frenetic, and each evening around 6 p.m. Malcolm Paris and I used to meet and see how much we could lend overnight on the money market, as interest rates for that short time span were very high. Things went from bad to worse, and we started to suffer a shortage of power as the strikes bit in and stocks of coal to generate electricity ran out; we went on to a working week with power three days one week and two days the next week. One evening, as I was just lighting my Tilley lamp, Malcolm called me to come and see him urgently. When I went in, he pushed some figures towards me, his hand shaking, saying, 'I think we're skint.' Our financial situation was indeed very dire – but so was P&O's; a mutual rescue package in these conditions was essential. Neville Vincent still distrusted Sanderson and his motives and put a private detective on his tail – plus sound surveillance and photography. I was aghast at this move, as I had to meet this 'Dec' at a different location every morning to get an update on Sanderson's activities.

Eventually, common sense began to prevail and we met up with our advisors and P&O and theirs, often with butane gas lamps and candlelight, to get a 'merger' together, as it was put, rather than a P&O takeover. Sandy Marshall of P&O was my usual contact, and we felt that we could do business together. We fell foul of the Stock Exchange and its regulations. They seemed oblivious to the fact that negotiating across the table, almost in darkness and with no electricity to power the typewriters, made things extremely difficult.

A deal was finally struck, the merger took place and the stock market viewed it with relief, rather than a reason to mark up P&O's shares. When I was at a candlelit meeting with Lord Inchcape and Sandy Marshall for P&O, and Neville Vincent for Bovis, just after the merger had been announced, we started to discuss and shape the new combined P&O Board. Naturally, Inchcape did not see much need for a great Bovis presence on the main Board, and as we went through all the Bovis directors, Neville finished up by saying to Inchcape, 'Oh, and we have a President.'

Inchcape replied that he thought that no such office existed, but asked who the gentleman was who was 'president'.

'The Earl of Albemarle,' Vincent replied.

'Good God!' said Lord Inchcape. 'Is he still alive?'

'Well,' responded Neville, 'it's very difficult to tell!'

As Bovis and P&O started to integrate, I began to be asked to advise the latter on legal matters and contracts; the economic climate at the time was still suffering badly from the Thatcherite confrontation with the trade unions and the stock market was weak, with the P&O share price in severe difficulty. I worked with Sandy Marshall there, and also with a most interesting personality, Oliver Brooks, as their Finance Director. Oliver, as I remember, was not a qualified chartered accountant, but had been Inchcape's factor on his estate in Glen Clova, in Scotland, and was 'brought in' to fill that office on Inchcape's insistence. He had lost a leg during the war, but despite that, he always rose from his chair, on his crutches, to greet you when you came into the room.

Oliver Brooks was seriously concerned about P&O's financial position at that time and also the low share price and stock market comment. Assets had to be realised, and it was decided that P&O's offshore supply fleet of some twenty-six vessels had to be put on the market to bring in some much needed cash before the end of their financial year on 31 December. Both Oliver and Sandy knew that I had previous experience of maritime transactions, and I was appointed as the lawyer to act on behalf of P&O, reporting direct to Sandy.

The fleet was managed by a really larger-than-life character, the cigar-smoking, hugely amusing Ray Kelly. An Irishman, formerly of the Inniskilling Dragon Guards, he was a very accomplished yachtsman, a bon viveur and enormous fun to work with. The prospective purchaser of P&O's fleet turned out to be Tidewater Marine, whose president, John Laborde, was a real hard-headed American businessman, based in Galveston on the Gulf coast of the USA. We had all the vessels for sale in one P&O company, but, on doing preliminary due diligence, Laborde refused just to buy the company, as he feared hidden contingent, possibly latent, undisclosed liabilities, and insisted that he would only buy each of the twenty-six ships individually. I can't say that I blamed him, as the ships were scattered all over the world on charter, and they were registered all over the place – Panama, Liberia, Bermuda etc. – and they were all 'hocked' to the eyeballs with marine mortgage debt. In addition, in some cases it turned out that ownership was split between various interested parties. I had always wondered why ship ownership is divided into sixty-fourths of a share, and now I was to find out.

Time was against us, and I hastily assembled a couple of other lawyers to help me: Basil Agapis, an Australian who had joined us, and Ron Wong, also on my staff. Negotiations were very tough, as what John Laborde was prepared to pay was a million miles away from P&O's aspirations; but he knew P&O were strapped for cash and that we had to close the deal by the end of the year. There then started a frantic series of surveys of all the vessels, located in Indonesia, offshore Nigeria, the North Sea and the Middle East. I brought in my wife, Ginny, to help out; she had been a first-class secretary in U Thant's office at the United Nations, and so was thoroughly organised and professional. Of the twenty-six ships, all had to have their existing charters novated to Tidewater Marine, all marine mortgages had to be discharged, and all ships' registration transferred and recorded in the country of flag registration. Ray Kelly was so relaxed and laid-back about the whole operation that our unofficial after-hours 'headquarters' became his mews flat, where the brandy and champagne flowed to ease our stress!

I had lawyers flying all over the place; closing was to be in New York on the morning of 31 December, and Ginny, Ray and I flew there the previous week to coordinate all that was needed. We had a hiccup with the Bermudan-registered vessels, so Ginny and I had to dash down there to meet with Conyers Dill and Pearman, the lawyers acting for us out there, and sort things out. We also managed a few hours enjoying a moped ride round part of the island and a superb seafood dinner.

The documentation required for each ship was horrendous and we calculated that we had to table 183 separate, completed and properly signed and executed documents on the table, in order to close the transaction to sell and transfer all twenty-six ships. Late in the evening before closing, Ginny, Ray and I were setting out the parcels of documents in our New York lawyers' office round a very large boardroom table when a secretary brought in a telex from Basil Agapis, whom I had stationed in Nigeria, to say that the crew of one of the vessels had mutinied, murdered the skipper and set fire to the ship… which had then sunk! So out of the twenty-six, I was one ship short, and I did not know what to do.

I have to say that by this time John Laborde and I had a good working relationship and when I called him in frantic fear that evening, as I knew his bank draft for £36 million had been drawn, he simply suggested that on completion, the following morning, I gave him an IOU to either refund the (agreed) value of the vessel, or supply Tidewater Marine with another ship of equivalent value! So we got the desperately needed funds into P&O's coffers before the end of the financial year on 31 December.

My wife and Ray Kelly flew back to London that evening, but as I had just heard that my father in Dundee had developed the early stages of lung cancer, I caught the overnight British Caledonian flight from New York into Prestwick. Arriving on 1 January, there was absolutely no transport of any kind available (as was common in these days in Scotland). However, the local aero club was operating, so I persuaded them to let me charter a Cessna 150, with the promise to return it two days later, and flew into the then grass strip at Dundee Airport.

When I came to turn in my expense report to Oliver Brooks for the New York trip, including going down to Bermuda, he 'bounced' the quite reasonable aircraft charter costs, as he said that I 'did not have authorisation to charter planes'. As I felt I had been instrumental in saving P&O, I was somewhat incensed at that, and it was one of the reasons that led me to believe that my future might lie elsewhere; there was always a degree of management friction between P&O and Bovis, and I did not feel that it was a happy marriage.

Iran

Having, as I said at the beginning, three daughters at boarding school at Beaconsfield, I decided that, before giving in my notice at Bovis, I had to find employment where some assistance for these fees was a part of the overall remuneration package – and that meant going abroad. So I became a regular reader of the 'Appointments' section of the major newspapers.

One day I spotted an advertisement for a Commercial Manager in Iran in the oil industry out there; the company was called the Oil Service Company of Iran, or 'OSCO' for short, and was run as a consortium company whose shareholders comprised most of the international oil majors, headed by British Petroleum (BP), with Shell, Texaco, Exxon (Esso), Total, Elf etc., right down to Getty Oil, who had a holding of one per cent. A largely BP-staffed company in London, Iranian Oil Services, or 'IROS', handled much of the offshore Iranian administration logistics and procurement, and it was they who had inserted the job advertisement that I had seen. I felt that my international experience with Bechtel and with the energy industries made me well qualified to manage the contract and procurement requirements for OSCO.

I was granted an interview by IROS and seemed to get on well with their Chief Executive, Jim Porter, and Peter Marshall, their Contracts Manager, and so my candidacy was put forward to OSCO for consideration. The Shah of Iran had recently decreed that the then present practice of just flaring off surplus gas at the well head had to cease and the gas, instead of being flared, either re-injected (to raise the oil table and increase recoverable reserves) or used as domestic gas, as Iran tried to modernise itself. That meant that there was to be a huge capital budget for construction projects, with very major contracts to be let, and that someone was urgently needed to come in and help to take that on.

When discussing the possible move with my wife, we had concerns over my previous experiences in the Middle East in Libya and Kuwait, but at that time, the Shah of Iran was an absolutely secure monarch, with the fourth most powerful army in the world, a strong economy and a stable regime. Little did we know what we were to ultimately live through.

I was duly asked to fly out to Iran for interview by the Chairman, George Link (Exxon), the Managing Director, Malcolm Ford (Shell) and the General Manager of Finance, Sidney Primrose (BP). While most of the expatriate staff were seconded from their parent companies, they did have acute shortages in certain areas – legal/commercial being one of them; so a number of 'direct hires', as they were known were recruited to fill the gaps.

My first hurdle arose when IROS informed me that I was the only one they would fly to Iran, and I would not be accompanied by my wife to see the conditions and the housing out there. Ginny, from her time at the UN, and her substantial overseas experience, either on mission or travelling with U Thant, was pretty streetwise, and I felt it essential that she should be present in Iran also; so I dug my heels in and was told that never before had a wife been flown out at interview stage. My reply was that there was always a first time. Then when the tickets came, they were economy, and I had to say that we did not 'do' economy – I think that I had a pretty exasperated Jim Porter at that stage!

We flew to Tehran and stayed at the Hilton overnight, and I went into the Tehran (OSCO) office to meet the people there, while Ginny was shown Tehran by a most charming Iranian on the OSCO staff, Mr Aboodi. However, there had been another Shah diktat that the senior management were to be based down in the area of the oilfields, and that the head office was to be in Ahwaz, with another office at the large oil refinery in Abadan near the export terminal at Kharg Island. That evening, we had the interesting experience of flying on one of OSCO's aircraft, a Fokker Friendship, from Tehran to Ahwaz. These venerable aeroplanes, even in those days, were very sensitive in their ability to climb high enough to cross the Zagros Mountains en route from Tehran to Ahwaz, and so not only did the luggage going on-board have to be weighed – but the passengers did as well. I was to discover later, in mid-summer, that from time to time somebody (usually the heaviest passenger) was 'shunted off' the flight.

We were met at the airport in Ahwaz, having flown over the oilfields and seen all the surplus gas still being flared off and unused. We were put up in the Astoria Hotel (irreverently known as the 'Ahwaz Hilton'). It was pretty basic, and one did wonder about the cleanliness of the kitchens. However, it had been a long day and we badly needed some rest. It was an early start for us the following morning, as the working hours in summer were 6 a.m. until 2 p.m. straight through, so there were cars at the hotel for us at 6.30 a.m. One of the drivers was to take me to the office for interviews and the other to take Ginny to meet one of the wives, who had been detailed to show her round and see the kind of conditions and housing available in Ahwaz itself. I was, by that time, a little nervous about what might lie in store. The OSCO offices were not far from either the airport or the hotel but one could see, on the way there, that this was a bustling small city set back in time and struggling to cope with the modernity of the oil industry that had landed on its doorstep, in those days managed and run by an expatriate 'occupying' population.

I first of all met George Link, the Chairman of OSCO, a charming, quite laid-back American with enormous experience of the Middle East, and we immediately found common ground when he learnt that I liked 'hunting and fishing'. He used to take a helicopter out at the weekends to go and shoot sandgrouse and wild boar, and spent his leave big game fishing off the African coast – so I felt that I had passed that part of the interview.

My most serious and searching sessions were with Malcolm Ford, the MD, whose great sense of humour and ready broad smile immediately convinced me that here was a man with whom I could work very well. He outlined to me the enormity of the task they faced in modernising the oil industry in Iran in such a short space of time, and the huge number of projects that had to be undertaken to build large Natural Gas Liquid (NGL) plants, major pipeline projects, gas re-injection, and also developing offshore oil reserves; I was staggered to find that OSCO had no less than fifty-one operational drilling rigs there, and the projected overall annual budget for implementing the Shah's requirements was $1.8 billion a year, which in those days was an enormous amount of money.

The way that OSCO was structured was explained to me. Most of the senior management were expatriates, although there was one Iranian General Manager, John Raoofi, and a senior manager of Engineering and Projects,

Bagher Mohammadi. Further down the line, there was a mix of expatriate and Iranian staff, as the goal was to gradually try to bring OSCO to be managed and run almost entirely by Iranians. To that end, the oil majors sponsored many Iranians to go to the UK and USA to take engineering degrees there.

I was also interviewed by Sid Primrose, the General Manager of Finance, a BP secondee from Scotland, who was the archetypal Aberdonian 'counter of the pennies', and we got on very well together. In the evening Malcolm and his wife Gwenda had kindly asked us for dinner so that Malcolm could spend more time assessing me, and Gwenda could form an opinion on whether Ginny would make a good expat wife. The following day I was given a quick trip by helicopter round the oilfields and some of the projects under way, and the following morning we were driven down to Abadan to catch a flight back to London – this time by Iran Air.

An offer of employment duly arrived at our home in Teddington, which, while impressive and generous in its terms, particularly with regard to school fees and a holiday trip to the UK and flying the children out twice a year, was disappointing in its base salary. I had come to the conclusion, during discussions at IROS and OSCO, that 'direct hires', as opposed to seconded oil company personnel, were classified as somewhat second-class citizens, and that the salary band for the same grade of job differed depending upon what category you fell into, and this I found unjust.

I had a discussion with Ginny and told her that I thought we ought to go back and say that the base salary was too low and that it should be increased by at least ten per cent if I were to accept the job. Ginny said, 'You are crazy, James! You will blow it, and we need the job for the school fees.'

However, I stuck to my guns, and wrote back that I would accept the position if there were a ten per cent increase. Jim Porter, the IROS MD, called me back the following day to say that the salaries were based upon a Hay MSL grading system and for my grade they were already at the top of the band. I suggested that perhaps, with the huge increase in contract work expected, it was the grading of the job that was wrong and that the position should be regraded to a higher salary band. During the days all this was going on, Ginny was quite sure that I had, indeed, 'blown it'. However, Jim Porter called a few days later to say that an offer letter was being posted out, on my terms, and could I confirm that I would accept it and when could I start?

I have to say that Bovis were very understanding about my decision to leave them, particularly as it was unlikely that, in the near future, I would have been offered a seat on the P&O Board, as the merger/takeover had been pretty acrimonious at times and negotiations had been very tough and direct. As is often the case in senior management, once you have decided to leave, it is often better for both sides if you clear your desk and go, so that you are not privy to any further plans for the company while you are working out your notice. I was delighted that Bovis insisted that I kept my Jaguar XJ6 as part of the termination package, as Ginny and I had both grown to love that car. IROS and OSCO were also pleased that we were able to bring forward our date for starting to work in Iran. And so a five-year saga began!

First Impressions of Iran

Although we had made a brief visit to Iran as part of our interview, we had not really had any opportunity to see much, or have any communication with local Iranians, so we were in for a very large culture shock on arriving.

We had – very wisely, as it turned out later – decided not to let our house in Teddington, but decided to have it available for my frequent business visits to London and for our home leave. So packing up to leave for Iran was more a matter of acquiring suitable clothing for the hot temperatures there, and also taking out my kilt evening dress and Ginny an evening dress or two, as we knew from our 'interview' visit there that the standard of dress for formal evenings was pretty high.

This time, we flew from Heathrow to Abadan in Southern Iran, with Iran Air – of which I was to become a very frequent passenger. The pilots tended to be either an American or European captain with an Iranian co-pilot, although on domestic flights, within Iran, nearly all the pilots were local nationals. This time, I am glad to say, we had been issued with first-class tickets without fuss – as I was now 'senior staff'. However, our first trip turned out to be something of a nightmare; on take-off from Heathrow, just as the aircraft had become airborne, it dipped and fell quite heavily on the tarmac before 'bouncing' back into the air again. After climbing as usual up to about 1,000 feet, it did not seem to me that we were taking the normal 'climb' pattern out of Heathrow, but just maintaining altitude, although the undercarriage had been retracted.

About five minutes after that, the flight engineer – they had one in these days – came out from the cockpit. I heard the flaps coming down, the aircraft slowed and I could hear the wheels being lowered. I said to Ginny, 'Something's wrong,' and the flight engineer proceeded to roll back the carpet in the aisle. Then with a torch he peered down some kind of inspection tube and then went back into the cockpit to report to the captain. He then came up on the PA system and in a very relaxed American drawl told us that 'we might have a small problem'. By this time, Ginny was clutching my hand quite tightly. He explained that a Lufthansa aircraft, lined up behind us for take-off, had seen our 'bounce' and thought that our port (left-hand) tyres had burst, so we were going to fly to Stanstead Airport and do a low 'pass' along the runway there with the undercarriage down in order that engineers there could take a look and assess whether it was just one tyre that had been damaged, or all four...

The carpet in our aisle was replaced and I suggested to a steward that I thought opening the bar was a good idea, as I felt the need for a stiff gin and tonic – to which he responded with some alacrity. We made two passes, on full flaps, and then veered off southwards. The wheels came up and more power was applied to put us back into a climb. The captain then came on the PA again and said ground staff had confirmed that, in all probability, all the port tyres had burst. He stated that we were about to witness a most unusual sight, in that he was going to fly high over the Channel and then dump fuel, as we were too heavy to make an emergency landing. He had been offered two locations, but preferred Heathrow, as they had the best emergency services. When we got over the Channel, the captain invited us to look out of our windows and witness streams of fuel coming out of the end of the wings; we were too far forward to see – so the best thing seemed to be some more refreshment!

We then turned back towards Heathrow, and as the wheels came back down (this was before the 'Brace, brace' era) our very calm skipper told us that as we touched down, the plane might veer on landing, he hoped just a little bit to the left, or maybe a little bit more, and we should be prepared to evacuate through the chutes and to leave all belongings behind. The ladies should remove their shoes.

As we approached the airfield perimeter, we could see a carpet of foam along the runway and fire engines racing down in parallel to us – a most comforting sight. That American pilot was absolutely brilliant; he came in with the right wing down at an angle until the starboard wheels touched, and held the nose wheel up as long as possible. Then that went down, and finally there was a horrible screeching noise as we clattered down on the rims of the four burst tyres on the port side. We did veer to the left – but not off the runway. The fire engines were there in seconds, but fortunately there was no fire, and after the wheels had been sprayed with foam and there was no risk, buses arrived and we were able to walk down the steps and on to the bus with our hand luggage.

When we arrived at the terminal, we were told to wait and an announcement would be made about what was to happen to us. By this time, Ginny and I were both starving, and I knew of a decent airport restaurant in a different area. So, on our own, we just headed off for that, as we considered it would take some time to either repair the aircraft or find a replacement – which we thought, with Iran Air, was unlikely to be available at Heathrow. As it happened, our dining table overlooked the airport, and astonishingly we could see our plane, which must have been towed in by a tractor, with engineers swarming round the offending wheels.

Just as our main course came, the engineers all suddenly packed up and disappeared; it was too far to see the state of the aircraft and we were worried that as we were in a different part, we could not hear any announcement as to whether we were to re-board. So we bolted our very expensive lunch and rushed back to the Iran Air desk, only to be told that our flight had been cancelled as the aircraft was too badly damaged. In fact we were rescheduled to depart around 11.30 a.m. the following day, and meanwhile we would be put up in a hotel.

We decided that, as Teddington was not far away, we would just go home, sleep in our own bed, and go back to the airport the next morning. Our neighbours were so surprised to see us back – all having said fond farewells the night before. We went up to our favourite Italian restaurant for a relaxing dinner and were pleased to see Arthur Lowe, of *Dad's Army* fame, at his usual table, as the series was being filmed at the nearby studios.

Setting off the following morning, we had the same American captain, who, after take-off, came on the PA and said, 'Well, ladies and gentleman, having given you the scenic tour of southern England yesterday, let's get down to the serious business of actually getting to Abadan.'

Flying in towards Abadan we could immediately see all the gas flares from the oilfields and the huge refinery at Abadan and the large tankers loading crude oil at Kharg Island.

The first thing that struck us on disembarking was the

really hot dry breeze, with a touch of humidity – *sharji*, as it was called in the Iranian language – something with which we were to become very familiar, as at certain times of year the humidity meant getting through three or four shirts in one day, and the use of a good deodorant was essential! We were met by a driver sent down from Ahwaz, where we were to be based, and driven up in the dark – a terrifying ordeal on the first occasion, with high speeds and huge lorries thundering down in the dust heading south to Abadan. It was just as bad as the crazy driving standards we had witnessed in Tehran, and I very soon learnt that the best thing was to have a newspaper held high in front of me so that I could not see the traffic, and just trust in the ability of my driver and the will of Allah!

We spent the first night revisiting the Astoria Hotel. There was always an odd smell of drains in the hotel, and the air conditioning was patchy and very noisy. Ginny and I did not get much sleep that first night, knowing that a car would be waiting to take us to the office at 6 a.m. the following morning – expecting us to have showered and had breakfast. As I have said, in the summer, office hours were 6 a.m. till 2 p.m. without any lunch break, and in winter they were 7 a.m. until 4 p.m. – but with an hour for lunch at twelve.

Our driver introduced himself as 'Alwan' and was an extremely courteous and good-looking young man. He seemed to be delighted that he was to be our driver, and over the years we got to know and like him very well – even though his English was poor and at that time our knowledge of Farsi was non-existent.

Ginny and I were then put through the usual personnel formalities to get all the required local documentation dealt with: photographs, passes, driving licence applications etc.

As most permanent oil industry staff from the oil majors did two-year tours, there was a high turnover of personnel, and the formalities of induction were very well rehearsed and thorough. Following this, we were taken to our temporary quarters in the residential area, where a small flat had been prepared for us, and our bags were brought round so that we could unpack and settle in. It was all hugely interesting and exciting, except for having to deal with a cockroach or two, as the flat had been empty for a short while. The two air conditioning units were quite noisy, but essential in the heat of the day in 30°C plus. We were to become quite used to the background noise, even at nights while sleeping, and it did drown out any external noise from traffic.

That evening, Malcolm Ford, the Managing Director, gave a dinner party for us, at which we were introduced to all the general managers and managers and their wives, both expatriate and Iranian – a somewhat daunting experience, but it went off very well. Both the expatriates and Iranians gave us a very warm welcome, and it turned out to be a very pleasant evening. We had our first taste of the ready availability of caviar, served in liberal quantities, accompanied by the local chilled vodka, followed by a chicken dish called *fessenjan*, which was slightly sweet to the taste, containing chicken, pomegranate, orange juice and spices. The rice was to die for and we asked how it was cooked. Sedi Mohammadi, one of the wives, had taken an instant shine to Ginny, and explained that the rice was boiled and drained. Then a bowl was coated in butter, the rice put in, and the covered bowl was put into a hot oven so that the outside of the rice became a crispy brown – a recipe we would recommend to anyone.

The following day, Alwan was waiting for me at 5.45 a.m. ready to drive me to my first day at the office, while one of the long-serving expatriate wives had volunteered to take Ginny under her wing and take her to the bazaar and staff store to start stocking up on groceries and provisions.

On arriving at the office, I was greeted by my Iranian Head of Contracts, a most charming man, Hooshang Ramhormozi, whom I subsequently learnt was married to an American former ballet dancer, Jill. Hooshang took me to my office, where I met my secretary, an Armenian girl called Manoosh, who immediately went to get us some tea, while Hooshang and I got to know each other. Next I was taken to meet all the other contracts and procurement staff in Ahwaz; many of the senior staff were expats, but as one went down the organisation they became entirely Iranian.

Hooshang already had a great pile of files on my desk for me to get stuck into, as it was apparent that there was a great deal of catching up to do in getting major projects off the ground in order to start fulfilling the Shah's decree that all possible flaring of gas should cease and that the gas should either be re-injected, converted into NGL (Natural Gas Liquids) or pumped into the rapidly developing gas systems being built by NGC (National Gas Corporation). It rapidly became clear to me that I had a huge job on my hands, and I was very glad that my time at Bechtel had got me used to dealing in large numbers, as many of the projects proposed ran into hundreds of millions of dollars per project. When Alwan drove me back to our apartment around 6 p.m., having been at the office since 6 a.m. I was extremely glad that we had brought a bottle of duty-free whisky with us.

Ginny had also had a most exciting day and found the sights and smells of the bazaar absolutely captivating, and as she already had a well-developed sense of bartering from her time on mission with the United Nations, she knew that she was going to be in her element. We spent that evening alone and struggled a bit to come to terms with the somewhat erratic water supply and the vagaries of a bottled gas cooker. However, we were there, settled in and life in Iran had begun.

We obviously had a great desire to learn to speak some Farsi, as, outside OSCO, little English was known, or spoken by the local Ahwazis; so it was off to Farsi classes either very early in the morning or in the evening, and we soon got the hang of the basic courtesies and the ability to tell our driver '*dasti rast*' (turn right) or '*dasti chap*' (turn left). We also had to get Iranian driving licences, as my driver was off at the weekend (Thursday and Friday), and we also did not wish to have him waiting too late for us in the evenings if we were out playing bridge or at a dinner party. Our 'driving test' was hilarious – consisting of a drive round Ahwaz with an examiner who spoke no English, and when it came to test our eyesight in the classroom, he made us copy him as to how many fingers he had pointing, and whether to the left, right, up or down – and we all passed!

Although senior staff had to stay in the middle of the oilfields in Ahwaz, about one third of my department were based in OSCO's Tehran office. The National Iranian Oil Corporation (NIOC), which was effectively our master, was based in Tehran, and many of the oil majors such as Shell had offices there also. So very shortly after my arrival, I flew up in one of the company's F27s to meet my Head of Contracts in Tehran, again a most charming Iranian, called Hassan Mohebbi, who was small, very dapper, a graduate of an English university and who immediately impressed me with his competence and dedication – but again seemed delighted to have a new 'boss' to whom he could relate. Hassan introduced me to the rest of the staff there, and we immediately began a very good working relationship. Hassan was an old hand but felt strongly that there was not enough control in the award and execution of some very major contracts. In his view, there was a perceived lack of 'check and balance', and the Engineering and Construction divisions were really too powerful and paying lip service to the contract procedures that were supposed to have been in place, and I immediately resolved to do something about that.

The flights between Ahwaz and Tehran were not without incident, as we had to cross the Zagros mountain range in either direction. I can't remember what the Fokker Friendship's maximum flying height was, but it was an unpressurised aircraft, and not only did we suffer severe turbulence, but I remember chunks of ice clanging off the hull as we struggled to gain, or maintain, altitude. As I was a qualified pilot (which became known to the aircrew), I was frequently invited to sit in the jump seat in the cockpit so that I could see what was going on! I remember that on one occasion the German skipper asked me if I had done a 'flaps up' landing recently (simulating the flaps being jammed), and as the strip at Ahwaz was three kilometres long he allowed me to take the aircraft in. This entails a much faster than usual touchdown, and some of my colleagues, knowing that I was in the front, were not amused as we rushed down the tarmac. George Link, the Chairman, carpeted me the following morning and told me in no uncertain terms that my job was to run Contracts and Procurement and not pretend to be a pilot! These trips were once or twice a week, and meant very long days.

Our major personal project as we settled in was to get our housing fixed, as we were in a temporary OSCO flat. It was quite cramped and had pretty cheap and battered furniture in it. This turned out to be quite an undertaking, as it was OSCO's habit to rent a property from a local Iranian businessman, a man who was definitely on the make as far as rent was concerned from cash-rich oil majors. With three children, who would be visiting during holidays, and given my grading, we were entitled to a largish house, and I stipulated that it must have a swimming pool. After much searching we came across a decent-sized house in a walled and secure garden, but it was in a state of considerable disrepair and still had Asian 'loos'. Also, the swimming pool had been disused for years. Getting the house renovated proved to be an extremely long-drawn-out, difficult and at times hilarious experience. The standard of workmanship was more like 'hit it with a hammer' than anything so delicate as tiling and grouting the bathroom.

Most of the supervisory work fell to Ginny, as I was in the office all day and could only inspect the daily 'damage' once the workmen had gone. As we neared completion, we watched with fascination as the workmen started painting the inside of the swimming pool; they started by doing the side walls and then started on the floor, painting from the walls inward and ended up in a tiny 'hole' in the middle of the pool, with wet paint all round them and no way to get out without leaving their feet covered in paint and foot-prints on the pool floor!

When we finally got the house finished, we had to set about furnishing it; we were given a reasonable allowance towards the cost of furniture, but buying it and getting it delivered was another matter; most of the craftsmanship was pretty basic, and imported furniture an impossibility due to the very high import tariffs. We discovered that the only thing that we could bring in tax-free were skis – as skiing was a 'Shah' sport and there were no manufacturers of skis in Iran. That was to come in useful later in providing my three daughters with new skis for Christmas.

What Ginny did love, with her adoration of Persian carpets, was finding carpets to lay on the tile floors, both in the reception and bedrooms. The Persian carpet traders were great fun, and although a great deal of haggling would go on over the price, the quality was excellent. They were itinerant traders, calling on the house from time to time and if we were undecided which carpet we liked best, they would leave one or two with us for up to six months, while we made up our minds which of the carpets we preferred. There was no question of our having to leave any deposit or anything, as we were trusted. Their psychology was, however, accurate in that they knew we would not have the nerve to say we did not like any of them – so they always made a sale.

Having finally moved in and got the pool commissioned with the help of a drilling company, we became very accustomed, quite quickly, to doing a great deal of entertaining – with whatever happened to be available from the OSCO staff store and the bazaar. As many of the direct hire staff, and some from the oil companies, were on single status, and there being nowhere to go apart from the golf/squash club, we felt duty-bound to look after them and give them a decent meal from time to time.

We also set up a games night, which was held on Thursday evenings. There being no English television (long before the days of satellite broadcasting), there was a necessity for one to make one's own entertainment. Bridge was very popular, particularly among the wives, as they were not allowed to work, and the days were long while their husbands were at work. So on games nights we offered everything from bridge and whist to Scrabble and mahjong, with copious quantities of beer and local wine, and a good time was generally had by all.

When the Rugby Five Nations Championship came on, we were a very popular household indeed. Ginny's father had come out shortly after we had settled in and, as a wizard electrical engineer, known all over the world for his Morse skills, acquired during the Second World War, he rigged up a dipole aerial on our roof with great precision so that we could get good reception from the BBC World Service – which was to be a lifeline to us later during the Iranian Revolution.

He also set up a large television set and video player for us so that we could watch tapes. I arranged with IROS in London that my father-in-law would tape-record the Rugby internationals at his home, take them into IROS at Finsbury Square on the Monday, and that they would come out in the Monday evening 'pouch' with all the other documents being sent to OSCO. On the Thursday evening, after a weekend rugby international, everyone, particularly the OSCO rugby club members, came round to watch the matches; people went to the most enormous lengths to avoid listening to any radios or seeing any newspapers that might let them know the results of any particular match beforehand – it was great fun!

Working for OSCO

As I settled into my new job, the enormity of the task before us all gradually dawned upon me. Compliance with the Shah's edict on ceasing to flare gas was a huge and expensive undertaking which meant that, in a very short space of time, we had to bring in the world's largest engineering contractors with major construction contracts to build the LNG and NGL plants and the massive pipelines needed to transport both the oil and the gas. This also led to the peripheral major expansion of local Iranian contractors, many of whom I got to know well, and they did have good standards, particularly in civil engineering.

The scope of the Contracts and Procurement Department was extraordinarily varied and fascinating. We let contracts to build roads, lay pipelines, build power transmission systems, schools and offices, housing, chartering aircraft, ships and helicopters, building vast projects costing over $600 million per project; we ran the fifty-odd drilling rigs at one time both on and offshore... you name it, we had to undertake it.

With the heavy drilling programme and the increasing use of locally employed drilling staff, we did have a few accidents, and at one time had one rig blow out, which caught fire and also another two blowing out of control and spewing oil onto the ground and gas into the atmosphere. A well head fire is a pretty awesome sight – incredible heat and noise. These 'blowouts' tended to be caused when the drill bit hit the gas cap at the top of the reservoir and the engineers were not quick enough to get on top of the sudden surge in pressure, and the BOP (Blow Out Preventer) failed to cope.

We had the famous Red Adair under contract to advise on these occasions, under a very lucrative arrangement, and he used to fly out with his two henchmen 'Boots and Coots', as they were known. Adair always liked the flamboyant; I remember that, with one of the rigs on fire, there was a small sand dune mound not far from the well head, and Adair's proposed solution was to fit a heat shield on the front of a JCB and put an oil drum, packed with explosives, in the front bucket. He would then drive the JCB as close to the flames as he could, lower the bucket and the drum would roll over the well head, explode and kill the fire by the debris smothering the well head. I am glad to say that this was not an option accepted by OSCO drilling managers. On another occasion, all the golf balls in Ahwaz were sought in order to inject these lower down the well, with the melting gutta-percha then sealing off the well – strange ideas indeed!

OSCO's normal practice was to put two rigs from different drilling companies at right angles to each other some way from the well head. They would then, in competition with each other, directionally drill down to the existing well, and when there was 'communication' immediately pump down a barytes-based sealant at very high pressure. There was a very substantial bonus paid to the drilling rig that got there first, and the beauty of it was that the well head could be replaced and the well was not lost – as it would have been with high explosives!

I once flew back on the same flight to London with Adair, Boots and Coots and I was aware that, instead of just changing planes there to go on to the States, they were asked to 'rest a little while' until they had absorbed the 'refreshment' they had consumed on the Tehran–London leg.

As I started to settle in, I became increasingly concerned, as I think I have said, about the way many contracts were awarded, and felt that the Engineering Group was too powerful in its ability to decide who was awarded what contract and on what basis. There were some contract procedures in existence, but these were more honoured in the breach than the observance, and I began a bit of a 'battle' with Bagher Mohammadi, the Engineering General Manager. I felt very strongly, as taught in my Bechtel days, that no single person should have the sole power to award major contracts. We did, supposedly, have a Contract Committee for contracts up to £1 million, and a Major Contracts Committee for contracts over that amount; but the contract department representation was weak and had been made subservient to the wishes of the engineering department.

So, with support from the MD, Malcolm Ford, I set about strengthening the contract award 'rules' and making sure that both Contracts and Engineering had to jointly sign off on any contract award recommendation before it went to the Contracts Committee. Then, if they could not agree, each had to submit a paper explaining why a particular award should, or should not, be made, so that the Contracts Committee could rule on their choice, on an informed basis. It was very gratifying to learn later that, as I understand it, Shell adopted many of these procedures worldwide.

I also suspected that contractors, both local and international, were operating a ring from time to time. We never tendered to more that six contractors for one job, but it would appear that they met and discussed, perhaps, whose 'turn' it was to do the next job. So they would take the base value of the job – say $5 million – and inflate it to $7 million as the lowest bid, the others all putting in higher tenders and then splitting the $2 million surplus between them! So to try to put a stop to this, we set up an independent Cost Engineering Group who were issued with tender documents just like all the invited contractors, and also had to submit a sealed tender as to what they had costed the project at. That certainly did throw up some astonishing anomalies and enabled us to re-tender the project with a sharp message to the bidders to get their act together. I sat on the Major Contracts Committee, to do battle with Mohammadi, and my Contract Heads sat on the lower committees in Tehran and Ahwaz. Keeping these matters clean in a country like Iran where 'baksheesh' was a way of life was not easy – as I was to learn later on.

The workload in the contracts department was soaring, with so many new projects starting. Keeping bid deadlines was under severe pressure, as well as running the myriad of contracts already in place: exploration, drilling, engineering, aviation, maintenance etc. – all needed administering. I managed to persuade Malcolm that I needed some more help at senior level, and so we created a second Head of Contracts for Ahwaz. I was very relieved when BP sent out Phil Watson to fill that post. He was highly experienced, had worked in Iran before and very quickly settled in, with his wife Freda joining him in Ahwaz. Hooshang and Phil worked very well together and took a great load off my shoulders, dealing with all the current contracts; this left me free to concentrate on the very large new projects coming up.

As the design and engineering work on some of the major contracts developed, we had a stream of the major international contractors rushing out to see us: Fluor, Parsons, Foster Wheeler, Bechtel, R J Brown and many others. I had insisted that whenever any of these major meetings took place, both Engineering and Contracts should be present, preferably alongside someone from Sid Primrose's (later Bill Williams') Finance Department. The days were long and in the summer, the air conditioning struggled to keep us cool even in just short-sleeved shirts and lightweight cotton trousers. With having to change shirts two or three times a day, it was fortunate that our houseboy was an excellent ironer!

Procurement was carried out by IROS in London, on OSCO's behalf, and in accordance with our specification; we saw the bid documents before they went out and the bid analysis when the tenders came back, so we did have some control and input as to who our suppliers were. As we moved on, international travel again became a large part of my life. I frequently had to fly to London for meetings with IROS, and we also had to travel for contract negotiations with the construction majors, so Holland, the States and Japan were frequently on the agenda. I became a 'regular' on the British Airways morning flight out of Tehran, so much so that the chief steward (those were the days!) knew exactly how I liked my eggs scrambled. I think that my boss, Malcolm Ford, thought that I made any excuse to get out of Ahwaz; but it was necessary to keep a grip on how contract awards were dealt with. To this day Malcolm still reminds me how he struggled to approve my expense report after a major trip!

The daily pattern of life was long and arduous – but also fun; we worked hard and we played hard. Because of the time change, particularly with the States, we often had to work long into the evening. Supposedly we were off for the weekend, on Thursday and Friday; but Saturday being a normal Iranian working day, I was usually (as were many of us) in the office seven days a week.

Before the days of email and fax machines our main mode of communication was by telex, and we had a telex room with a bank of about twenty machines, all staffed by female Iranian operators; little did I think at the time that I would end up with an award as a telex operator!

Despite the long working hours, there was a great deal of social activity, well supported by the expats, and one never really missed the absence of television. Many regularly played bridge, and Bob Henderson, our BP doctor, ran painting classes, which first got Ginny into becoming a good amateur artist. We had a golf course – sand fairways and tarred greens – and there were also squash courts at the clubhouse, which were reasonably air-conditioned, so I kept fit by becoming a regular player. It is a wonderful way to exercise thoroughly over a short space of time: thirty or forty minutes of dashing round the court, followed by a shower and a few cold beers to replace the lost fluid – great fun. We also had the 'Hash House Harriers' for jogging and had a rugby fifteen in the winter.

We had a choir, run by Francis Chute of BP, and Ginny and I both joined; Francis produced miracles with our mediocre voices and our concerts and carol services were always very well attended, and it was a joy later to sing in our Cathedral Choir, once we had returned to Scotland. I took to teaching Scottish country dancing in the winter months, which went down very well with both expats and local Iranians – building up a class of over sixty. The main highlights for the Scots (and we had many of them) were St Andrew's Night and Burns Night; people almost literally fought to get tickets and, of course, they were full black tie, kilt evening dress, with ball gowns and tartan sashes for the ladies. The haggis and smoked salmon were flown out to us by British Caledonian, together with the pin meal with which to make Atholl Brose (the Highland liqueur); I remember coming home one evening and finding the four or five ladies who had been concocting the liquid had certainly overdone the 'tasting' and were well away.

There had to be a Chieftain for the evening – or several, as it sometimes turned out – as the Chieftain had to drink so many toasts with the various senior guests of the oil companies and the contractors. These toasts consisted of the obligatory 'swallow in one' from quite a sizeable quaich (silver cup), and as one Chieftain slid under the table, the next reserve had to take over. On the occasion that I was Chieftain I did survive the whole night – but only because I had my bottle diluted with a little ginger ale! People spent hours on their speeches and addresses, and I don't think that I have heard a better standard anywhere else in the world.

We also had an exhibition Scottish country dancing eight, whom I tutored, and they performed various dances at both Burns and St Andrew's Night to a very high standard.

Life moved on both at work and play, with the children out for Christmas and summer holidays, and us back in Europe skiing at Davos at Easter.

We badly needed new and more spacious offices, and before my arrival, NIOC had approved a budget allocation for that purpose. It was way out of date but we were told that it could not be increased. As the first round of tenders came in to our design, all the bids were way over budget. So I brought in a firm of Scottish architects, Reiach Hall Blyth, and sought their help as to how we could achieve the working space we badly needed, within the budgeted parameters that we had.

I arranged for them to develop a modular design with standard offices and open-plan areas, and suggested that we framed the tender in an entirely and, as far as I am aware, unheard of way. We took the budget sum, discounted it by a safety margin for contingencies, and then sent tenders out asking how much office space we could have for the fixed price that we gave them. This caused some consternation among those invited to bid, but after receiving visits from all tenderers and explaining our strategy, we did get in some excellent international bids. The best of these offering us the most office space was Dragados, based in Madrid – so that became a frequent city to visit in order to hammer out the final details of the contract. Their hours of working were punishing; we met at 8 a.m., worked until about 2 p.m., then had lunch with them and retired for a 'siesta' in the heat; met again at 6 p.m. and worked through until about 10 p.m. Then, we were entertained at a very late dinner, complete with flamenco dancers etc., and it was about 2 a.m. before we got to bed – only to be up again at 5 a.m.!

Keeping Things Straight

While we had little knowledge, or time, for Iranian politics, we were aware of the Shah's absolute dominance of the country and his iron rule. We knew and had heard of Savak, the Shah's secret police, and we were aware that any challenges to his regime were ruthlessly dealt with. Opponents to his dictatorship were imprisoned in the notorious Evin jail in Tehran or, worse still, just disappeared.

We also became aware that it was suspected and subsequently confirmed that OSCO had Iranian Savak staff that had infiltrated as staff members. They were all qualified for the posts they filled. I tried to discuss this with my Iranian managers and heads of department but they were very reticent about discussing it. Although I was meant to be running Contracts and Procurement, and should have had control over who my staff members were, from time to time people were just 'posted' to us by NIOC, and we had to accept and integrate them into our staff organisation.

We also had extreme difficulty in tackling bribery and corruption, which was rife and a way of life in Iran. For example, one day I found an Iranian civil contractor sitting in my office when I arrived back from another meeting; I think that he had bribed his way into the office, as he had no appointment. I knew him quite well and agreed to see him. He apologised profusely for disturbing me, but when I asked him why he needed to see me, he said, 'Mr Lawson, I am finding it difficult to continue working for OSCO as it is costing me so much money to get my invoices paid.' I asked him what he meant by that statement and he said, 'I am having to pay 100,000 rials cash to get an invoice paid. It has been said to me that Mr Ford [the Managing Director] gets 50,000 rials, you get 40,000 rials and your staff get 10,000 – and that is just too much.'

I was completely taken aback by this remark and assured him that neither I, nor Mr Ford, would be party to any such impropriety. I examined him closely as to how these cash payments were made and promised to look into it and investigate thoroughly.

So I got hold of my Iranian Head of Contracts, Hooshang Ramhormozi, and we began an investigation as to how and when and to whom these payments were being made. It transpired that when invoices were submitted, they were sent first to an Iranian contract analyst whose job it was to check that the invoice was made up in accordance with the signed contract rates for the contract, and that the calculations and the amount payable were correct, before passing it to Hooshang for endorsement and then to me for approval/endorsement or approval by Malcolm Ford, depending upon the value of the invoice. It transpired that this contract analyst had told the contractor that he had instructions not to process the invoices unless there was an envelope handed to him with the 100,000 rials in cash, so that the payments previously mentioned could be paid!

We tracked this person down as being a Mr Latifpour and I had him brought to my office and confronted him with our evidence and told him he was being dismissed. Getting rid of Iranian employees was not an easy matter, but I was so furious about this that I persuaded Personnel that he had to leave my staff immediately.

To my astonishment some eighteen months later I found this Mr Latifpour sitting in a chair outside my office, and when I approached him he said he just had to see me and that it was very, very important. As I told him that he must leave at once and get out of my office he said, 'But, Mr Lawson, I need my staff appraisal for my time with OSCO. I am due for promotion, which will include a car for me and my family, so it is vital that I have it.'

I told him, in no uncertain terms, that he would get no appraisal out of me and to get out of my office at once and never come back. He looked at me desperately and just as he was leaving I said, 'By the way, what are you doing now that makes you need this appraisal?'

'Oh, Mr Lawson, I am with the National Iranian Gas Corporation (NIGC), and I am Head of Internal Audit.'

I suppose the theory was that it takes a thief to catch a thief!

Early Signs

It was early in 1978 when we really began to see increasing unrest and opposition to the Shah's regime developing, mostly in Tehran and the holy cities of Qom, Isfahan and Shiraz, which were where the mullahs wielded enormous power and influence. The Shah was trying to modernise Iran and move it towards a contemporary European way of life and standards, while most of Iran was still at least a couple of centuries behind that. It was always astonishing to fly out of Ahwaz, as the centre of the oil industry, with electricity, air conditioning, street lights and tarmac roads, and pass over or visit so many villages that were still leading a very basic life with none of these benefits and no power, decent housing or any operational infrastructure at all.

They knew of the decadence of Tehran, the riches of the oil wealth and yet had continued suppression and lack of local investment. It was a country divided into two – the few who 'had' and the many who had nothing. The resentment, increasingly fomented by the mullahs, was growing.

Returning to 'baksheesh' for a moment, we had the Shah and Empress Farah Dibah coming to open a flagship NGL plant shortly when it was revealed that a vital piece of equipment, essential to the start-up (and which had been specially machined and delivered from the States as a one-off) was missing. Panic set in, as the Shah's visit was imminent along with all the pomp and ceremony that went with it. Miraculously, it was whispered to us that if we went to souk number eleven in the bazaar we might be able to find such a part. It cost us 500,000 rials to get it back – but the plant was started up by the Shah on the due date!

I was still travelling frequently, working particularly on the development of the offshore sour gas field, the Pars Project, and so was passing through Tehran, London and Tokyo, and thus had access to assessments of the gradual deterioration and unrest with the continuance of the Shah's regime. On one such trip, on my way back, I joined my wife, Ginny, at a hotel in Cyprus for a spot of leave. It was then that we heard on the BBC World Service of the commencement of student demonstrations and rioting in Iran. I remember to this day Ginny turning to me and saying, 'James, this is the beginning of the end.'

The day before we left, we heard that martial law had been imposed in twelve cities, Ahwaz being one of them. We flew back to Athens, and because of the almost nation-wide curfew newly imposed in Iran, all flights into the country were severely delayed or cancelled. After a twelve-hour delay at Athens, we managed to get a flight to Tehran, and after a further delay of five hours at Tehran airport, eventually flew back to Ahwaz, where curfew was, at that time, 9 p.m. to 6 a.m.

Shortly thereafter, the curfew was relaxed to 10 p.m. and then 11 p.m. Although there was much unrest both around the university and in the bazaar, with frequent reports of rioters being killed, we, in the residential districts, were almost trouble-free as far as rioting was concerned.

However, shortly thereafter, OSCO's Iranian staff started to go on strike and bring the day-to-day working life (and production from the oilfields) to a complete standstill. All the banks in Ahwaz were also on strike, the PTT (telephone company) was on strike, and many shops closed – either in sympathy with the strikers, or more usually because they had been threatened that if they remained open their shops would be bombed. The teachers also went on strike, and all schools were closed. All perishables or fresh fruit and vegetables became even scarcer, and we had to rely increasingly on the OSCO staff store – which was extremely erratic in what it did or, more usually, did not have.

For me, and the other expatriate managers and staff of OSCO, trying to carry on the day-to-day running of the business became a nightmare. The striking employees, which included each and every Iranian employee below management level, could not have been more uncooperative, and life became extremely tense and difficult. Pay cheques were not being processed, and with all the banks on strike, it was impossible to pay invoices to contractors or write personal cheques. The strikers could be found grouped in the corridors of the OSCO offices, and it took little to provoke them.

Japan

We did our best to carry on as normal, and our negotiations with pipeline bidders for the massive sour gas Pars Project were coming to a head. I was asked to go to London for meetings with IROS and then on to Japan to finalise negotiations with the preferred Japanese bidders, and if not successful, go to see Mannesmann in Germany, or Vallourec in France (British Steel having totally failed to meet the stringent technical specification required for the pipe).

I decided to take Ginny with me as far as London and give her a short break from the increasingly stressful situation in Iran; this would be about the end of October 1978. Then, after meetings in London, I flew on to Tokyo with our Pipeline Manager, Derek, and the IROS Procurement General Manger, Ken Snooks.

That trip is worth recording in itself, as an insight into contract negotiation and what can be achieved. We boarded the plane to Tokyo at Heathrow, and in these days we flew 'up front' on long-distance flights and we were ushered to our first-class seats, towards the rear of the cabin. It looked to us as if the (high-backed) seats in front of us were unoccupied, but when the pre-take-off champagne and canapés arrived there were obviously passengers there.

After take-off, and when the seat belt signs had been switched off, surprise, surprise, the three London office managers of the three Japanese trading houses involved in the bid (whom we knew and had already met) stood up and came over to us, bowing, and one of them said to me, 'Hello, Mr Lawson – what a wonderful surprise that we are all on the same flight! It is very good to see all of you.' It was an indication, with more revelations later, of just how good the Japanese intelligence was!

On arrival at Tokyo Airport, we had already been told on the plane by the trading house managers that transport had been arranged to take us to the Okura Hotel (they knew where we had booked in) and, sure enough, there waiting for us were two large black limousines with white-gloved chauffeurs, and we were told that they would be at our disposal twenty-four hours a day for the duration of our visit. We had already decided that the cars might be bugged, and so did not discuss any business at all or negotiating strategy during the drive to the hotel.

The following morning, after breakfast, we did have a meeting in my hotel room to discuss tactics, and how we were going to tackle the very large gap between their bid price and OSCO's budget. We were then driven to the offices of one of the trading houses, where a veritable phalanx of representatives of the three steel mills and three trading houses were assembled – possibly about thirty, and only three of us. All seemed to be aware that this was to be possibly the largest ever single order for high quality sour gas pipeline in the world.

We started with a detailed review of the Japanese bid, as many points needed clarification – both technically and commercially, as well as the quality control and delivery schedule – and we were able to repeatedly infer that sections of the broken down bid price were unreasonably high and unacceptable. It was a very long first day (still suffering from time change jet lag), and we broke up to return to the hotel – only to be told that cars would collect us at 9 p.m. to take us to dinner as guests of the trading house hosting the meeting that day.

So we showered and changed and were duly driven off for dinner at a geisha house where, after removing our shoes, we were ushered into a dining room with a long low table (about eighteen inches high), where the older Japanese men who had been at the meeting were present. They came forward and bowed and ushered us to sit on the floor cross-legged at the table – with the three of us opposite the three most senior Japanese. Then there walked into the room some of the most stunning geishas, who came and knelt down beside each one of us, bowing first and smiling graciously. They were there, apparently, to feed us. Conversation was very limited as very few of the older Japanese spoke English, and quite a bit of translation had to take place with an interpreter at the end of the table – a formidable female dressed in a black kimono.

When the first courses arrived of spring rolls, sushi etc., I started to reach for my chopsticks, being very grateful that I had become adept with these from my many visits to Japan when with Bechtel. However, the most delicate little geisha appointed to look after me smiled and shook her head gently, picking up the chopsticks. She was there to feed me herself! I quickly got the hang of it. The geisha would wait until I was ready and then she just popped the food in when I turned towards her and opened my mouth. There were liberal quantities of sake and Suntory Japanese whisky available – but at least I was able to control my intake by being allowed to lift my own glass!

The next course was a great Japanese delicacy, Kobe beef; this is the meat from a special breed of cattle, who have been fed bran from malting barley, taken little exercise during their life and indeed massaged to produce the tenderest of beef. Small charcoal braziers were put on the table surrounded by a bowl of a boiling liquid. The geishas picked up small slices of beef with their chopsticks, cooked the beef and allowed it to cool a little, before just popping it into your mouth – it was quite delicious!

When the fruits arrived, lychees and such, a tall geisha entered the room; she turned out to be a magician who did all sorts of tricks with scarves and silver rings. At the end she came over to me, as the senior guest, amid applause and presented me with a small wooden box. As I was looking puzzled, she signalled to me to open it – and inside was my right sock! How that trick was performed, I know not to this day.

By this time, some of the younger team had come into the room and we were told that we were now being taken for 'some entertainment', so bang went the prospect of a decent night's sleep.

Outside the geisha house, there was a row of black limousines with white-gloved chauffeurs standing by each car, and we were ushered in and driven off to a nightclub some thirty minutes' drive away. On entering the establishment, we found we were obviously expected, and there was much bowing and scraping by the staff as we were ushered to a large table not far from the stage and dance floor. We had obviously, either previously, or while we walked in, been 'sized up' as to our height as, while we were standing prior to being seated, a bevy of the most beautiful Eurasian girls in kimonos came over to us, each taking the arm of whichever one of us was nearest to them in height. Champagne and canapés then instantly arrived, and my right hand was constantly held and squeezed by my gorgeous hostess, who had some basic English – I think that her name was 'Kuomo'.

Very soon, as the sake and Suntory whisky, and then the champagne, began to take their effect, we were on the dance floor, dancing to Western music, with my hostess always smiling and swaying sensually with the music, and at times holding me very closely. After some time there was a bleeping noise from the back of my hostess's kimono belt, and she excused herself. I asked one of our Japanese colleagues why she had gone and he laughed and said, 'Don't worry – she will be right back, I have just signed her up for another hour!' It appears that these hostesses were provided on an hourly basis, and the charge added to the bill. My 'Kuomo' returned and nuzzled up even closer to me, if that were possible.

By this time it was about 2 a.m., and what with the jet lag, the negotiations and the hospitality, I was ready to go back to the Okura Hotel for some badly needed sleep. I then noticed our pipeline expert, Derek, on the arm of his hostess, leaving, and was told with a wink by one of the Japanese that he had 'elected to be taken care of'. It became clear to me that these Eurasians were probably more than just hostesses, and that you had to make it clear if you did, or did not, want to take matters any further! So I gently told our hosts that Ken and I wished to leave.

There was some delay as the company credit card was produced and then the 'madam' came back with the chit to sign and a huge wodge of Japanese yen. After the signature by our host I saw the cash divided between him and the 'madam'. I gathered, later, that it was standard practice for these trading houses to double the bill at the nightclub and split the excess in cash. Our black cars were waiting for us outside and we returned to the hotel for what was left of the night.

I had organised that we would meet for breakfast at

7.30 a.m. and then have a strategy session in my suite at 8.15 a.m. before the cars picked us up, to see how this huge price gap could be broken down. Derek did not appear at breakfast, so I telephoned his room and asked him to get to my suite immediately. We were greeted by a walking wreck as Derek shuffled in, his clothes dishevelled and his toupee at a crooked angle. He obviously had a severe hangover. I poured him black coffee and asked what had happened.

Derek said that there had been a black car and chauffeur waiting for him and his hostess and that they had been whisked away to a small 'hotel', where he had to take his shoes off at the door. He was led by the Eurasian into a room with a heart shaped bath and bed and joss sticks burning in candlelight. He was undressed and put in the bath and then she came in beside him and scrubbed him all over with scented soap, got him out, dried him and took him off to the heart-shaped bed. He did not remember what time he left, but only that the chauffeur was waiting for him and took him back to the hotel.

During our strategy session, we had debated whether to call IROS to say that, as the other bidders were higher, and the gap with the Japanese so large, an increase in our budget was essential, otherwise we were wasting our time. There were some numbers quoted in our discussions, and it was later to become a salutary lesson as, when we resumed our discussions, one of the Japanese mentioned a possible compromise contract figure – which could only possibly have come from our rooms being bugged. Thereafter, Ken and I agreed that any and all discussions we had on tactics would take place in open ground outside.

Thursday wore on with more detailed commercial and technical discussions and the gap narrowed slightly; but we still had a gap of over $60 million between their adjusted price and our budget. That evening, it was the turn of the second steel mill and trading house to take us out, and again the chauffeured cars were there. This time, it was the best, most expensive French restaurant in Tokyo, and again, the older Japanese men entertained us first.

We had the most fantastic dinner with Grand Cru Classé wines, and it was a pleasure to sit at real tables with proper chairs and our shoes on, although conversation was some-what stilted as, again, few of the older Japanese spoke much English. As I feared, as dinner drew towards a close, in walked the younger team, and our hearts sank as it appeared it was to be yet another nightclub. We were, again, whisked away in the black limousines, this time to a different nightclub – but we were obviously guests of honour and shown to a large seating area. Thankfully, there were no Eurasian 'escorts' provided for us this time, as there was a floor show and several other acts.

After some time a chair was placed in the middle of the stage and a man came over to me, bowed and asked me to sit on the chair; he then gave me a cigarette and asked me to light it and put it between my lips. He then retreated some distance and I could hear this whirring noise as he swung a thin rope with a small weight on the end of it round and round in circles. He then went down on his knees, and every time the lead weight whirled round it became closer and closer towards me, and I could start to feel the breeze caused by air passing over the weight. Then the man suddenly lunged forward and I will never know to this day whether the weight knocked the cigarette out of my mouth or whether it fell out through sheer terror! We did not stay on much longer after that.

The Friday morning we were back at the negotiating table, and after a very hard slog we had reduced the gap to some $46 million between our budget and their contract price; but we seemed to be at an impasse. During the lunch break I spoke with the senior leader of the Japanese team and told him that, at their final price, we were not going to make it. I asked him to call his secretary and get her to change our booked flights back to London on the Saturday to Düsseldorf instead. We broke off the whole session early on Friday afternoon, our having already called London to have it confirmed that no increase in our budget would be accepted. Because of the break-up of the talks and negotiations, we were left in peace at our hotel that night and had a quiet, somewhat despondent meal on our own; we were all pretty exhausted.

We had arranged to have breakfast together before going out to the airport on Saturday morning, and while in the middle of our meal, the senior Japanese negotiator came across to our table and bowed and asked if he could speak to me privately.

I went out into the lobby with him and he said, 'Mistaah Lawson, we need to talk to you – we are here to talk again.'

I said, 'What, all of you?'

He replied, 'We have conference room in hotel and we are all ready – would you and your colleagues please join us after you have finished your breakfast?'

I said that we would – but that we had to leave quite shortly for the airport.

I went back to Ken and Derek and told them what had happened, but we agreed that we had nothing to lose, having finished our discussions, in going in to meet them again. We went into the conference room and, as one, they all stood up and bowed deeply and we sat down, with me in the middle of one side of the table. Ken was on my right and Derek to the left. There was a pause while coffee was put in front of us, and after a tense silence the lead Japanese negotiator stood up, bowed again and said, 'Mr Lawson, gentlemen, we do not wish you to travel to Germany, so we have kept your flights to London today; we have had discussions and we agree that we will meet your price.'

Ken, Derek and I were quite astonished – that was a price reduction of $46 million!

After we broke up and our London-bound tickets were handed back to us, Gogtoh, the lead negotiator, came over to me and said, 'James' – using my Christian name for the first time – 'we could never have let this major project leave Japan and lose to Germany or France.'

Champagne was immediately produced, and it was smiles and handshakes all round – I just could not believe that such a huge reduction in negotiation could have been achieved, and that we were coming back with a pipeline purchase order within the NIOC budget!

I know that the line pipe was delivered, and lay for many years on a dockside in Southern Iran – and I now know that the Pars offshore field was eventually developed.

Some of the Japanese team insisted on coming to the airport (Narita) to see us off and ensure that we were not troubled by Customs, and I was handed a small soft parcel, which was put in my case unopened. We boarded the British Airways flight back to London very tired, but extremely content.

My wife Ginny, who, as I have said, had come as far as London with me on our way out and stayed in our house in Teddington, was at Heathrow to greet me. When we got home and unpacked my case, the parcel contained the most gorgeous length of pure Japanese silk in midnight blue, which Ginny had made into an absolutely stunning dress.

The Beginning of the End

I had been 'cocooned' as to what was happening in Iran while I was in Japan, but Ginny had been listening avidly to every news broadcast on the subject and it was clear that matters were going rapidly downhill. There were an increasing number of riots, strikes and arson attacks, and much anti-American and anti-British feeling – as both the USA and Britain were still publicly supporting the regime of the Shah.

I stayed overnight with Ginny in our house in Teddington and the following morning – this was late October – we shut the house and set off for Heathrow, our friends and neighbours somewhat doubtful about the wisdom of our returning to Iran. Our driver, Alwan, met us at Abadan Airport. He appeared very tense and apprehensive and desperately anxious to get us back to our home in Ahwaz before curfew, and it was a nightmare of a journey in the dark with huge trucks thundering down upon us in the opposite direction on the single-carriageway road. We just made it, and were so delighted to be reunited with our two lovely cats, Dimple and Haig, whom our usual house-sitter had kindly looked after and fed during our absence.

On going into the office the following morning, one could sense the increased tension, and we listened to the BBC World Service every morning to get reports of what was happening in Tehran and other cities. I had immediately called my Iranian Manager in our Tehran office, Hassan Mohebbi, as soon as I got into the office (we had a direct line PAX system, independent of the national phone network). He was extremely guarded with his information, but I gathered that the unrest at the universities in Tehran was increasing, that violence was spreading and that Savak, the Shah's secret police, were being pretty heavy-handed with anyone showing dissent with his regime, and that people were, literally, 'disappearing' into the notorious Evin prison – never to be seen again.

I flew up to Tehran from Ahwaz the following Tuesday on the company plane, and the atmosphere at Mehrabad Airport was entirely different. Normally we were treated as VIPs and Mr Aboodi simply walked us past Passport Control and Customs – but this time it was very different. Our passports were checked and rechecked, and our bags searched and the attitude of the Iranian staff was patently hostile to all expatriates.

In the office, Hassan apologised for being so muted when we had talked, but he was afraid that perhaps our microwave phone system was being monitored or bugged, and as an Iranian, fiercely loyal to OSCO, he had, nevertheless, Iranian friends and relatives who were absolutely sure that matters were going to get worse, and that expatriates, particularly American and British personnel, would be a major target, as Britain and America were so publicly and forcefully supporting the Shah's regime. On the way back to the airport that evening we could see damaged/burnt buildings, and a huge police and military presence; it gave me a grim sense of foreboding as to what was to come.

Back in Ahwaz we still tried to keep a sense of normality; we still had our Thursday games night for those expats on single status; we had also started rehearsals in the choir for the Christmas carol concert, and I still taught Scottish country dancing at the golf club once a fortnight, and managed the odd game of squash.

During November, however, the unrest shown in Tehran and other cities began to manifest itself in Ahwaz. We began to see notices on expatriates' cars telling them to leave Iran, and also notices in some of the offices. For example, I came into my office one morning to find my paperknife stabbed into my desk with a piece of paper on which was scrawled, *Leave Iran or you will be kiled* [sic] – not a comforting message at the start of a day!

The trigger for extreme unrest spreading to Ahwaz appears to have been a speech on television by the then British Foreign Secretary, David Owen, strongly supporting the Shah. This received wide coverage on Iranian television and the following day at the OSCO offices all the walls were bearing stuck-on handwritten posters such as 'Dirty British pigs – go home' and 'Yankees get out' or 'Owen is a puppet of the Shah'. That evening we gave a dinner party for the British Consul, who was visiting Ahwaz from Tehran and was the guest of honour. I felt compelled to hand the Consul a letter, on behalf of all British expatriates in Iran, saying how very much David Owen's speech had damaged our relationship with our Iranian colleagues, whom we worked with every day. The Consul assured me that its contents would be passed to the Foreign Office.

Later in November Ginny flew to Cyprus with a friend to try to buy a small property for us there. The banks were still on strike, so travellers' cheques were unobtainable (this was before the days of multinational credit cards). I had to plead with the OSCO cashier to release some Iranian rials, and as this currency was rapidly becoming unacceptable in the world, one of my loyal Iranian staff kindly went down to the bazaar to a money changer the night before she left to get pounds sterling – which were widely accepted in Cyprus.

Two days after Ginny went to Cyprus, Iran Air went on strike, and my proposed business trip to London, flying out from Abadan, became impossible. I was due to join Ginny in Cyprus for a few days' break on the way back. Fortunately, I had always kept my very good contacts with Bechtel, who were very active in Kuwait, and Jolly Dwyer, their Regional Manager, managed to get a Bechtel plane into Ahwaz and flew me to Kuwait. From there I got a commercial flight to London, where we had a series of very important meetings to finalise the details of our contracts with the Japanese. Ginny was becoming ever more fraught with worry in Cyprus at the deteriorating situation being reported in Iran. After my London meetings I flew to Cyprus for a few days before flying on to Athens, then to Tehran on an Olympic Airways flight, and from there to Ahwaz in the company plane.

As soon as I got back, Jolly Dwyer of Bechtel called me and said that they needed to get their ten Americans based in Tehran out of there, but could not get permission to send the plane to Mehrabad Airport. With some arm twisting with our own OSCO flight management, we managed to get clearance to get the Bechtel plane into Ahwaz where it refuelled and then took off for Tehran under a flight plan filed by OSCO. Fortunately, the aircraft was unmarked – apart from its registration number – so our little deception was never picked up. Jolly Dwyer was over the moon when the Bechtel Tehran-based team arrived safely in Kuwait, and we vowed that we would meet up one day for one hell of a party!

As November wore on we saw the situation deteriorating even more, and curfew was reimposed with increased hours of confinement. The army were, at that time, still professing loyalty to the Shah, and we had groups of soldiers stationed at strategic points round the expatriate residential areas and around the offices. There were so many Iranian staff in the field going on strike that production of oil and gas started decreasing. Paul Grimm, of Texaco, was Operations General Manager. A tall, well-built man and a huge presence, he was determined that production should be kept going, and started sending out normally Ahwaz-based expatriate engineers to take over from the Iranian strikers and keep the oil flowing – an action which infuriated the striking field staff – and several acts of sabotage took place, or were suspected.

Then, one November morning, when George Link of Exxon, our Chairman, was leaving his house to go to the office, his driver had stopped to shut the gates of the driveway when three young men rushed over and one of them threw an explosive device into the open door of the car and rushed off. George saw the bomb and immediately leapt out of the car and started chasing the youths. That act probably saved his life, as the bomb exploded, the car was wrecked and the driver, who was still nearby, was injured. As I remember, Exxon pretty immediately sent a plane in from Saudi Arabia and pulled George and his wife out, and as far as I am aware he never came back.

At the end of November, I had to make yet another business trip to London to IROS, and among other things report to the IROS boss, Jim Porter, and give him an accurate 'on the ground' report of the deteriorating situation for him to feed back to all the oil companies who were shareholders and anxious about the security of their crude oil supply. I worked very closely with Peter Marshall, the IROS Contract Manager, and one of his team, Fred

Williamson, as all the major contracts that we undertook were split with an 'inside Iran' contract for the construction and commissioning with OSCO and an outside Iran contract with IROS for the engineering design and supply of materials. I lunched with Fred, as usual, at Whittington's Restaurant in the City, which was a favourite watering hole of ours and I remember Fred's concern about where it was all going to end up.

I had brought Ginny with me, as I did not wish her to be alone in our house while I was away, and it was an opportunity for her to see her father. I also hoped that she might stay behind in London when we went back, but being the most loyal of wives, she insisted that her place was at my side, and that she was also concerned for all the other wives out in Iran and wanted to be with them.

A Warning

We flew back to Iran on 5 December on an Iran Air flight
(they were back flying again on the Shah's orders) and our
flight was from Heathrow to Abadan, via Paris. When we
boarded the plane – Ginny was unfortunately flying
economy – I saw that there was only one other passenger in
front of me in first class. After take-off and when the seat
belt sign had been switched off, he got up and came over to
me and greeted me by name, and I recalled that he was the
Managing Director of one of the larger Tehran-based
Iranian civil engineering companies who did work for
OSCO. During our conversation, he asked if I was getting
off in Paris, and when I said that my wife and I were flying
on to Abadan, he became very agitated and said that on no
account should we consider going back, as it was unsafe to
do so. He said that he was getting off at Paris to pay his
respects to Ayatollah Khomeini (who was at that time
resident in Paris) so I knew where his loyalties sat!

Ginny had, by that time, been invited up to the first-class
cabin with me. I was very reluctant to get into a political
discussion with this man, but it became obvious that he was
very pro-Khomeini, and told us that his father and other
relatives had been wrongfully imprisoned by the Shah and
that he felt very bitter towards him. He also told us that
Khomeini was receiving over $2 million a day from sup-
porters. Little did I know that this contractor was to figure
again in our lives!

We arrived in Abadan in the early evening and our

driver, Alwan, was there to meet us. Again, he was very nervous and was clearly anxious to get us back home to Ahwaz and our house as quickly as possible, and certainly before curfew. As usual, it was a pretty grim journey. As soon as we got home, Ginny rushed to see our two cats, Dimple and Haig, while I poured us both a very stiff drink.

Back in the office the following morning, it was clear that life was becoming even more difficult and crude oil production was being seriously affected. Gradually, the strike spread from the oilfields to the offices, and younger and junior staff began to defect – although most senior Iranian managers, mine included, stayed loyal, and we sort of continued life as if it might all go away: bridge, games night, squash and choir practice and amateur dramatic rehearsals all stubbornly went ahead within the limits of curfew.

Just after our return at the beginning of December, the very sad period of mourning in Iran called Assura started and it was announced that all shops and offices would be closed for a five-day period from the Thursday. It was expected that there would be much rioting, but Ahwaz was strangely quiet – although no less than an estimated 3 million people marched through the streets of Tehran in relatively peaceful demonstrations in support of Khomeini. We had all been advised during that period to stay indoors, either in the house or the office, and not to form any large gatherings. By this time we were receiving no newspapers, either national or international, and the daily half-hour news bulletin in English on local television had been stopped. Our only source of news and information was the BBC World Service, and how thankful we were that Ginny's father had fitted up that dipole aerial on our roof, which gave us excellent reception.

We had a brief lull after Assura, and staff trickled back to work. The telex machines (our lifeblood with IROS and our shareholders and international contractors) were still working. Oil production continued, although nowhere near back to its normal levels. However, we did hear of rioting down in central Ahwaz, and also news of renewed rioting in Tehran, with universities closed by the Shah and public buildings being set on fire.

Then, around 15 December, things got worse and the rioters from downtown marched upon the OSCO main office, chanting and shouting. All the Iranian staff were ordered by the rioters to leave, in the name of the 'Revolutionary Guard', and it got very menacing indeed as it appeared that it was the rioters' intention to set fire to the building. I think it was John Raoofi, our senior Iranian General Manger, who had alerted the military to the situation, and all of a sudden a squadron of Centurion tanks rolled up and surrounded the rioters – with their machine guns pointed in a circle in towards them and our offices. My office had its window on to the front forecourt, and I was beginning to get very nervous about what was going to happen next. I heard the tank squadron commander start to talk to the rioters and they became quiet. How I wished I had been more diligent in attending my Farsi classes! But I did get the gist of it. He was ordering the crowd to disperse, and I could see the gunners clutching their machine guns and looking very threatening.

Finally, the officer gave them an ultimatum that they had to disperse in three minutes, otherwise he would open fire – my Farsi was just about up to understanding that, as I could see him looking at his watch and counting out the time – and I did know my Farsi numbers!

Below my window there was a two- to three-foot

concrete sill so I got down and lay along that as the countdown went on. It got to ten seconds and then I clearly heard the countdown to zero. By this time, far from retreating, all the rioters had sat down with crossed legs and held each other's hands. It was quite astonishing. This was their chance to die for Allah and enter the promised land as martyrs, with the gift of a promise of forty virgins. They were completely silent. When the countdown finished I really expected to hear the command to order 'Fire!' You could have heard a pin drop. Whether the officer was considering his future loyalty to the Shah, or whether he lost his nerve, I shall never know. After what seemed like an age of complete silence (probably only about a minute) as one, the crowd just stood up and walked away chanting, '*Allah Akhbar!*' (God is great) repeatedly. I have to say that my concentration, until it felt safe to leave the office, was non-existent – I had been absolutely terrified!

The following day we had a meeting of senior expats in the office to discuss the situation. A couple of senior military officers were also present, who assured us that we would be protected in future and that steps were being taken to ensure that. The next day, early in the morning, as I was shaving at home before going to work, we heard this loud rumbling noise and the clatter of tank tracks. When I had dressed and gone outside the gate of our walled garden, there, in the middle of the road, right outside our house, was a fully armed and manned Centurion tank, and I could see a row of them spaced out all the way up towards the office. So our protection had arrived. I left the house as normal and sure enough, we had a military presence the whole way to OSCO's offices.

As we struggled on under these conditions, life became very difficult for the expat wives; they could not go down to the bazaar in safety and the OSCO staff store increasingly had very little to offer – eggs disappeared, flights bringing in imported chicken and beef stopped, vegetables were almost non-existent and alcohol very scarce indeed. I think that Ginny did get out to Kuwait for a day's shopping trip with one of the American drilling company's planes – but with Christmas coming up, that went straight into the deep freeze. However choir practice etc. still went on within curfew – now well established.

On 20 December we heard that saboteurs had blown up a main pipeline at Gachsaran at 9.30 p.m. The point of blast was a confluence of three lines near a bridge. It would have had a devastating effect and could have interrupted production of the entire Gachsaran oil production if all three had been ruptured, as was probably intended (App. 1).

On 22 December, a delegation of about ten Iranian staff delivered mass resignation letters from 540 individuals, citing reasons for their actions (App. 2). Matters were now deeply serious – and worsening.

Then on Saturday, 23 December, as Ginny put it, 'the lid blew off'. At 6.45 a.m., our good friend and my colleague, Paul Grimm of Texaco, the senior American General Manager there at the time, was driving himself to work, rather than using his driver, when he was brutally assassinated at a roundabout on the way to work by two gunmen with Kalashnikov rifles. Paul usually had his driver to take him to and from work, but it was his habit at weekends to drive himself home on Wednesday evening and drive himself in to work on Saturday (the beginning of the working week). Paul and his wife, Burdeen, had had lunch with us the previous weekend and we had discussed his vulnerability driving the car he had – general managers and the Chairman had large black limousines which easily stood out – and I had played squash with him only two days before he was killed. Paul's body was not removed from his car for several hours, but the British OSCO doctor confirmed that he had died instantly (App. 3).

The news of Paul's assassination swept through the office and the whole expatriate community like wildfire, and everyone was shocked and appalled by this dastardly and brutal attack. I got one of my staff to go to Ginny to tell her to stay at home. The next twenty-four hours were a long nightmare spent trying to arrange for Paul's body to be flown back to the States before Christmas, with Burdeen accompanying his body. Tom Evans was, by then, the senior American General Manager, and he, John Raoofi and I had a great deal to do to persuade the authorities to move quickly, the situation being complicated by the fact that Customs were on strike and his body had to clear Customs before being allowed to leave. John pulled out all the stops, and I do know that we had to pay considerable 'costs' in rials to achieve this (App. 4).

With the earlier attempt on George Link's life and the assassination of Paul Grimm, the American expatriates, particularly the Exxon staff, felt that such was the anti-American feeling, even hatred, that they had to leave at once – and urgently. A telex expressing the fact that conditions were 'not acceptable' was sent out to IROS to be relayed to Exxon on 24 December and received by IROS at 6 a.m. UK time (App. 5). A further telex was sent out from Ahwaz at 5.10 p.m. the same day (App. 6), saying that forty-one family members and three employees (proceeding on 'early leave') were to be flown out from Abadan by Gulf Air at approximately 8.30 p.m. that same day. They were flown down from Ahwaz to Abadan in two F27s organised by OSCO's Head of Aviation, Captain Cameron. IROS and

Exxon had clearly moved fast to get these people out so quickly. Little did we know at the time that this was to be the first of many Gulf Air 'rescue missions'.

The following day the telex facilities at OSCO in Ahwaz were bolted up and there was no one prepared to go in and operate them. We were left with no operational telephones internationally and no telex.

A Frightening Experience

As a result of the seriousness of the situation, it was decided that there would be no parties or public gatherings of expats over the Christmas and New Year period. On Christmas Eve, the planned carol concert, for which we had rehearsed so hard, was cancelled. Morale was very low. To try to salvage something out of Christmas, Ginny and I went out to dinner to some friends living five streets away, Gene Muehlberger and his wife.

At this time curfew was still 11 p.m., and we arrived home just before five minutes to eleven. I got out to open the carport doors into the walled garden and as I did so I saw Dimple, one of our two cats, sitting in the middle of the carport. We always shut our cats in the house when we went out in the evening, so we knew that something was wrong, and with Paul's recent death much in mind, I told Ginny to stay in the car while I went to investigate.

As I approached the house I heard the crunch of a foot-step on broken glass. Going round the side of the house, after finding the front door still locked, I could see that the kitchen window had been smashed and opened. I just caught the shadow of a man with a rifle moving back into the darkness, so I fled back to the car, shutting the carport door on the way, and shot back to our friends' house to explain what had happened.

We knew there was a military guard post at the end of our street so Gene, our big tall 6' 6" American driller friend, came with me and we drove up towards it. By this time it was after curfew, so we were greeted by six soldiers, very nervously shouting to us to stop, and all pointing their rifles straight at us. We both got out of the car with our hands up and tried to explain that we knew that we were breaking curfew but that there was an intruder in my house and that we wanted them to come with us and investigate. By the time we had made ourselves understood, and after much chattering on their radios, a captain arrived who spoke some English, and we were escorted by him and his troops back to my house.

Somewhat nervously, I went to the house with the captain, who called out for whoever was in there to come out – but there was no response. So I opened the front door and the soldiers went in to find, not unexpectedly, that the intruder had gone. Our bedroom had been completely ransacked and was an awful sight. I asked the guard captain to go with Gene to his house and get Ginny and to post a sentry outside our house for the night.

Ginny's look of horror when she saw the devastation in our bedroom was entirely justified; every drawer had been pulled out and the contents tipped out and strewn every-where. We lost Ginny's jewellery, including my Christmas present to her – a gold bracelet that I had had made for her locally. I had only collected it that evening, and to hide it from Ginny had folded it into one of my kilt socks – but they found it nonetheless. Ginny also lost her gold Dunhill lighter and gold pen, pencil and biro set, an unopened bottle of perfume and about $2,000 worth of foreign currencies, which we had been hoarding because of the striking banks.

It was, of course, a sickening sight to come home to on Christmas Eve, but we felt that it could have been worse. At least all our silver was safe and our Persian rugs. I had obviously disturbed the intruder, as there were signs that he had tried to make his escape through the bedroom window. Both the cats were in a highly nervous state, especially Dimple. The kitchen was littered with broken glass everywhere and there was blood on one of the walls – presumably the intruder had cut himself on the broken window. All the kitchen cupboards, too, were ransacked, but the first thing Ginny checked there was whether the turkey was still sitting in the (switched off) oven! We were to be eight at lunch the following day.

So then and there around midnight, we set to, tidying the place up. I boarded up the broken kitchen window and started on the kitchen while Ginny tackled the bedroom; she felt that everything had been defiled so she changed the sheets and pillowcases on our bed and insisted on washing all her underwear, as she felt it had been handled and could not bear the thought. We slept in the twin room that night with the door locked and the cats in with us for what little sleep we did manage; the intruder could easily tear down the cardboard I had put over the kitchen window, and as I shut up for the night there was no sign of the so-called 'sentry' who was meant to be at our gates.

On Christmas morning, we went first to visit Jimmy Paton and his wife; Jimmy ran a company who supplied direct hire personnel to OSCO – Spencer & Partners. Jimmy was a larger-than-life Scot and his house was nicknamed the 'Scottish Embassy'; he was one of the few expatriates who still had a working telephone line. We had passed a message to my daughters to telephone us there from England, but sadly no call came through.

We then went on to our friends, Doug and Jean Jakeman, for pre-lunch drinks, before returning home. They too were having a very unpleasant time. They had received a threat that their house would be bombed either at

10 p.m. on Christmas Eve, or on Boxing Day. When they had returned from being out to dinner the previous evening, everything had appeared normal. They had been assigned a rather aged military guard. About twenty minutes after their return home, the guard had rushed in to tell them that there were five men on their roof. The guard called up his unit, but it was some time before reinforcements arrived and by that time, as they approached, the men had fled. Some time later, one of the men returned and was caught and arrested – and he turned out to be a young Iranian working in Doug's department at OSCO.

Our six guests arrived for lunch on Christmas Day, though neither Ginny nor I felt much like celebrating Christmas. However, we were glad that we had not cancelled as it at least made us forget the previous twenty-four hours. Apart from the miracle of producing a turkey with all the trimmings and Christmas pudding and mince pies, we had saved up some decent wine brought in from various trips, and I had developed a knack for producing a 'fake' port. The staff store usually had Bristol Cream sherry, and I mixed it with one of the better Iranian red wines and it made a really passable tasting 'port'. I always smiled when we had overseas top brass visiting us and they congratulated me on serving such a 'superb' port! By the end of the meal we were all relaxed and forgetting our situation and had a hilarious game of charades before our guests left to be back home before curfew. We still had a Centurion tank parked outside our compound.

The following morning three of us took one of the company F27s for a flight to Tehran. We were advised on our PAX microwave radio link that the British Ambassador to Iran, Sir Anthony Parsons, wished to speak with us urgently. On arrival at Mehrabad Airport in Tehran we were driven to the British Embassy through scarred streets, showing signs of fires and looting. The meeting was brief – but somewhat daunting. We all knew and felt that, following the attempt on George Link's life, Paul Grimm's assassination and the strikes and rioting, the continuing presence of expatriate personnel down in the oilfields was an increasing risk. However, that had to be balanced against the enormous investment made by the major oil companies to secure supplies of crude oil from Iran.

I immediately understood the problem that Sir Anthony had; I had met him before and had a profound regard for his ability and professionalism. He explained the situation to us very succinctly and accurately; it was this: both the United Kingdom and America had come out strongly in support of the Shah and his regime, insisting that Ayatollah Khomeini (still then in Paris) posed no threat to the Shah's future, or his regime. Having said that, he explained that, therefore, neither the US nor the British Government could issue any advice to expatriate personnel or their employer companies to leave Iran. Further, if our employers did decide to try to get us out, there was no way that either the US or British Government could assist or support an evacuation, either in civilian or military terms and that we were 'on our own'. He finished by saying that he wished to go off the record and said, 'The British and American Governments are supporting the Shah and we will be publicly stating that all expatriate staff need not leave Iran – but for Christ's sake, get your people out of here.' Later, I learned that a similar message had been delivered to IROS in London by the Foreign Office.

We had a very sombre and bumpy ride back from Tehran to Ahwaz; it was not a happy trip home. I immediately went to see Tom Evans and John Raoofi to discuss what to do next.

There were three or four people in Paul Grimm's department still trying to keep production going, and we felt that they would be key targets, so we managed to get clearance to fly an F27 to Kuwait the following morning. There was one spare seat on the plane and an OSCO employee (Shell), Otto Selis, had asked me if there was any chance his wife could get out with their two cats. So, with them in a holdall, Linda was able to get out of Iran with her beloved cats – sadly, not the same fate that befell ours.

Time to Leave

We now really had a crisis on our hands, as we had no contact at all with the outside world. Our international calls had been shut down and our telex room with a bank of about thirty telex machines was also very firmly bolted and shut, and international telex lines weren't working anyway. My office and personal phone at our house had been cut off. All we had was the PAX microwave link to our Tehran office and the Shell office there – stoically manned by a superb young lady who stuck to her guns to the very end and, I was delighted to learn, was later awarded an MBE. I spoke to her frequently and she was always calm and an efficient 'fixer', and I am ashamed that I cannot remember her name.

Tom Evans called a meeting that day with senior expatriate staff and John Raoofi, as the senior Iranian General Manager, was also there, and in his position obviously had good information about was likely to happen in the future. The strikers in the office and the rioters downtown now felt, strongly, that they were 'in control', and oil production stopped. The consensus, at Tom's meeting, was that it was essential that all wives, children and non-essential personnel should be evacuated as soon as possible, reducing staff to just a small core of a couple of managers and some engineers to ensure the safety of the operational plant.

The question was how? We had had no contact with IROS for over a week, no phone connection or telex, and had been clearly told by Sir Anthony Parsons that we would get no help, either civilian, or militarily, from the British or American Governments. I went home that lunchtime in an extremely despondent mood. We had set up a 'warden' arrangement, with various managers tasked with looking after all the families in their areas, as communications were virtually non-existent. Cliff Lucas was our warden and dropped by to see how Ginny was faring and with news of the fact that an evacuation was on the cards, if it could be organised; how, or when, was anybody's guess.

We were also provided with a personal military body-guard after the events of Christmas Eve. One of my Iranian staff had offered to go down to the bazaar to buy me a revolver, but it was felt that it might exacerbate the situation if it became known that I was armed. So a guard we had. The first one was a small private, who slept on a mat near the front door and was highly nervous.

That night, about 3 a.m., we heard a loud rumbling noise, and all the Centurion tanks guarding our residential area and route to the office had lumbered off into the night, and the guard posts disappeared too; this was the beginning of the Shah losing the loyalty of his troops and the start of their defection.

Mike Hall, the OSCO Personnel Manager, who had been at Tom Evans' meeting, had asked if Ginny could help him out and he came over to our house. He had various things to dictate that needed typing urgently and were too confidential for any Iranian staff that might still be working. These were the contingency plans for evacuation of expatri-ate employees, and also a list of instructions to be circulated to all expats. These instructions advised that no one go out after dark; that curtains should be drawn as soon as any lights were switched on; that we should sleep with some form of weapon under our beds; and that people should vary their routine, i.e. not leave their house at the same time each day, and vary their route to the office.

I had been wondering overnight about how we could possibly get an evacuation underway when I remembered that we had what was at that time a state-of-the-art satellite telex link, highly secure, in a little 'cubbyhole' just outside George Link's office, operated only under lock and key by George's personal secretary. I knew that this was called the 'eyes alone' telex, and enabled George to communicate with IROS – and via them, all the member oil companies – without the risk of the message being monitored or intercepted, as was the case when the normal telex system was used.

After I had left Mike Hall with Ginny and saw her using her immaculate Pitman's shorthand, I went into the office and called Anoosh, George's secretary, at her home from his office and asked her to come in and help me with the private telex. Anoosh told me that she would like to help but that if she did come to the office, she would not be allowed in by the 'pickets' on the door, and that she was too frightened to try. She did, however, tell me where the key to the 'eyes alone' telex room was, and I went into George's office and her workstation just outside and found the keys. On getting into this tiny room – about ten feet by six feet – I saw two telex machines, side by side, both apparently switched on and with no incoming telexes there. As I had not the first idea how to operate these machines, I locked the door and went back home to fetch Ginny, as I felt sure that, as a former secretary in U Thant's office at the United Nations, she would know.

I took Ginny into the office and up to the first floor and we went into the telex room. Sadly, Ginny had little idea, as these were completely different machines from any she had occasionally used. At that moment there was a knock on the door, and Hooshang Ramhormozi told me that the pickets/ self-styled 'revolutionary guards' knew that Ginny was in the building and was 'strike-breaking' and had to leave. She was escorted out of the building and driven back home. Meanwhile, I looked at these two machines and then, on a one-fingered basis on the left-hand machine, typed in:

'Hello – this is James Lawson at OSCO, is anybody there?'

I found a key called 'Send' and then waited for ten minutes or so, but there was no response. So I then went and sent the same message on the right-hand telex and sat back and waited. To my astonishment, a few minutes later, the left-hand telex burst into life! It was IROS and it started chattering out print. (Bear in mind we had had no communication with the outside world for about seven to ten days.)

'Mr Lawson, good to hear from you. Can we help?'

It then dawned on me that the right-hand telex machine was obviously on 'Send' and the left hand one on 'Receive', so I went to the right-hand one and said:

'I do not know how to operate a telex – please instruct me.'

Back came the reply: 'What make and model is it, and what is the serial number?'

The light in the cubbyhole was bad but I found a plate at the base with the make and model, but could not read the serial number and relayed back what information I did have. There then began an astonishing relationship between the IROS Head of Telecommunications and myself.

After that I was sent an 'Idiot's Guide' as to how to operate the telexes, and so it was time to get down to serious business; it was cramped and stuffy in the cubbyhole, but I felt that I had to keep the door shut and locked in case any

Iranian or self-styled 'revolutionary guard' came in.

Jim Porter, the IROS MD, then sent me a telex that a decision had been taken by the consortium of oil companies that all non-essential expatriate personnel, with women and children first (there were quite a few children visiting Iran on Christmas leave), should be evacuated, and that IROS were working on plans as the best way to achieve this. Getting out via Tehran using what commercial flights were still operating was ruled out. Airline offices there were already besieged with people desperate to leave, some Iranians included, and we were looking at over 1,300 people to move out in a hurry.

I told Jim, by telex, that we knew that Abadan Airport had been abandoned, with a complete strike of all staff, but that, geographically, it was an ideal location for us, as we could fly people down in the two F27s and two Twin Otters from Ahwaz to Abadan, as it would be too dangerous to travel by road by that time. The one piece of common sense advice I did have, as a pilot, was that any aircraft coming in to get us out would have to have 'self-start' capability, as there would be no ground power units (GPUs) available to start the aircraft's engines (App. 7).

When I had heard from Jim Porter, I went straight over to Tom Evans' office, and with Mike Hall there and several others, told him that evacuation was on, but quite how was not yet finalised. Tom set up a team to organise who should go out first, and the logistics of how many F27 and Twin Otter flights would be needed to make a planeload down to Abadan. I had guessed, correctly as it turned out, that the Boeing 737 would be an ideal aircraft, as it could carry about 130 passengers, but more importantly it had a tail-mounted generator, which could start up the engines one by one and so make it entirely self-sufficient.

There then began, for me, a wearing and tiring stint of being entirely alone in that telex room for up to eighteen hours a day. Once we had made contact with IROS, we knew that our evacuation was being planned as a matter of great urgency, as rioting was escalating and the situation destabilising by the hour. I went home that night, before curfew, elated that we had made contact with the outside world, but gravely concerned about how it could all be put into operation.

I went into the office the following morning and immediately logged on to IROS, having previously agreed that they would send no telexes unless I was there, in case the room was broken into and our messages planning the evacuation intercepted. Ginny, bless her heart, sent me off well provided with sandwiches, a Thermos flask and water. As our phone was by this time cut off, she was very concerned, and I urged her not to be alone but to visit friends, or that I would arrange for Cliff Lucas, our warden, to call round and check on her and give her any news.

Gradually the evacuation plan began to take shape; IROS had reached an agreement with Gulf Air that they would start to fly in planes (737s) in two days' time and start to get OSCO expatriate personnel out. There was serious doubt whether they would be given landing rights and air traffic control clearance, and that became a major worry. Tom Evans, John Raoofi and I discussed this, and John then left to try to fix it. It transpired that there would be no objection to the Gulf Air planes coming in, but there would be no formal clearance and no air traffic control staff in the tower at Abadan Airport, and that they would have to fly in VFR (Visual Flight Rules) and that there would be no ground staff assistance at all. I had no knowledge what the contract was between IROS and Gulf Air to fly in and get us, but I imagine, given the risks, it must have been very expensive. I left that evening, knowing that we had to get the first passenger manifest out to IROS the following morning.

Cliff and Pat Lucas had asked us out to pre-curfew supper and a game of bridge, so I quickly showered and changed and we went up there. Just before we left, Mike Hogg, one of my contract staff, came round to the house and said there was a very urgent message for me to call a number in Tehran. He gave me a slip of paper with the number on it and said he did not know who had asked to be called. As our phone had been cut off since 17 December, and we thought that Pat and Cliff's phone was still working, as soon as we got there I called the Tehran number. I picked up the phone and the conversation went something like this:

'Mr Lawson, you will remember me when I tell you that we were together on a flight to Paris recently, when I was getting off there to pay my respects to Ayatollah Khomeini and you were flying on to Abadan, which I told you was dangerous. You are well liked and respected by the Iranian contractors as being a fair man, but you are not safe in your house and you should leave Iran as soon as you can. If I tell you that your cats saved your life two nights ago, you will appreciate just how serious the threat to you is. They know that you are involved in organising an evacuation and that you are regarded as a major target. I am very sorry, but we cannot control all that goes on in Iran; you have to leave as soon as possible because it is not safe for you to remain here.'

I have to say that I was pretty stunned to get that message and a cold shiver ran down my spine. All I could think of to say was something like 'It was probably just a burglary', but the contact told me that as the intruder was in the house, he had taken what he could. This might explain why only items that would go in pockets had been taken. He also said that he knew our telephone had been cut off and that this was no accident, and that all expatriates' phones were systematically being cut off, and then he hung up.

I went back into the room and told them all what had happened and relayed the gist of the conversation. Questions came flooding in. How did he know about the cats? Who was watching us? Should we go back home at all? I am afraid none of us had the stomach to play bridge, and Cliff insisted on following us back in his car and seeing us safely back home. Our guard was still there, but looked most unhappy in the job he had been given.

We went to bed and at about 3 a.m. there was an almighty crash. We leapt out of bed and I went into the sitting room and then to the hall to find the guard very nervously doing up his tunic and reaching for his rifle. The sound had come from the kitchen with the broken window, and I had to literally push the guard in front of me to see what was up. It transpired that the cats, Dimple and Haig, had decided they were hungry and opened the cupboard where they knew their food was kept and had knocked a metal bowl on to the stone floor! The guard was visibly trembling, but relieved, so we made him a cup of tea and we went back to bed and tried to get back to sleep – not an easy thing to do, and it showed how on edge both of us were. Our guard was replaced next day by a young sergeant. He arrived with some pretty horrific tales of dead bodies lying in the streets and cars overturned and set on fire in the main part of the town.

The following morning, 28 December 1978, I was up at 6 a.m. and off to the office with my 'rations' for a long stint in the telex room. We had pre-arranged with IROS that they would have telex staff in by 4 a.m. their time, and that was when the evacuation plans all really began to take shape. Tom Evans, Mike Hall and Jerry Gilbert had been working on who should leave Iran first, and I had wanted Ginny to stay on for a bit, but we came across the problem of some wives refusing to leave without their husbands. This became a bit of a nightmare and tensions were high. I suppose I had sort of emerged as the senior Brit, as I was so involved with the evacuation, and so it was agreed that wives would literally be ordered out, whether they liked it or not. So, as an example, I had to put Ginny on the manifest of the first passenger list.

One of my young lawyers, Graham Wedlake, and his partner, Sue, were in a very exposed part of Ahwaz and for safety, as we had a guard, they were going to move in with us in Kien Pars. It would have been company for Ginny, as she was still very concerned about my safety, following the phone call about the cats saving our lives. Graham, like others, was making himself useful as a part of the warden service, keeping people at home up to date with what was going on.

Graham and Sue were a delightful, fun young pair, and had come to work for me in a very unusual way. They had been walking and climbing in Kathmandu and had pretty well run out of money when they got to Tehran. As I recall, they had gone to the commercial section of the British Embassy and were pointed in the direction of our Tehran office. As it happened, I'd just had to dispense with the services of a lawyer from Shell who had been sent to me without my having had the chance to interview him, and I soon learnt why he had been made available at such short notice. Not only did he come into his office with an electric griddle and have a fry-up when he arrived in the morning, but there was always a bottle of vodka in his desk drawer, which I discovered when I became suspicious.

Graham became what was know as a 'direct hire' rather than an oil company employee and I decided that it would be better to have him in Ahwaz, rather than Tehran, where his predecessor had been. On moving them down, we hit a snag when it was discovered that they were not married, as OSCO rules strictly forbade any unmarried couples occupying company houses. So we had set about trying to get them married in a hurry; but it proved extremely difficult, and we were just about to get them married by an Armenian priest when the evacuation loomed up. They became known as the 'unwed Wedlakes', and have remained friends of ours ever since – indeed we are godparents to one of their children. They did get married when they got back to the UK.

Back in my 'cubbyhole', I encountered a major problem in that there was obviously suspicion in IROS in London that I might not be who I said I was, and that an Iranian operator might be there and then relaying all the details to the Revolutionary Guard, so that we would be walking into a trap.

The Telex chattered: 'What is your full name, date of birth and OSCO registered employment number?'

I was extremely puzzled by this, as I had been operating the telex for quite some time – but I replied anyway. Then came: 'When you are in London there is one person whom you always meet and you go out to lunch together; please name that person and give the name of the restaurant that you go to.'

I replied: 'Fred Williamson, and we have lunch at Whittington's Restaurant in the City.'

That seemed to satisfy them in London and they

apologised but said they thought the checks very necessary. Later in the day IROS advised that Gulf Air had agreed to fly into Abadan with 737s but they could not tell us when the first flight would be, although we should have the first planeload of passengers identified and ready to move down to Abadan.

Tom Evans and Mike Hall gave me the first passenger manifest, and I laboriously typed this out on the 'Send' telex; as a two-finger typist it took me an age. We were also advised that Gulf Air would fly the 737s from Abadan to Bahrain. There the evacuees would transfer to TriStars to be flown to Athens, where BP was booking hotels and sending out staff. By the time I had got the manifest typed, sent and acknowledged by IROS, it was late, and I went home absolutely exhausted. We were having regular power cuts by this time and it was horribly frustrating to have to sit and wait there until such time as the power came on.

As can be seen from App. 8, we went to pretty desperate lengths to try to have conversations with London so that we could report verbally on the situation, our plans ahead and our views on security. I also had a personal problem in that, after a post-operative thrombosis and two DVTs, I was permanently anticoagulated and was desperately short of warfarin (the poison used to kill rats!) to keep my blood thinned down. The locally manufactured drug was useless (having previously ruptured my kidneys), and in any event the pharmacies were all shut. I urgently needed to get some flown out to me in 1 mg and 3 mg tablet form. So, in one of the phone calls, I asked for the warfarin to be flown out to Athens, given to Gulf Air to take to Abadan, and then be flown up to Ahwaz in an OSCO plane – quite complicated logistics!

On Their Way at Last

When I went back into the office at 6 a.m. on 29 December, I was sent a telex asking me to contact IROS immediately. When I did so, I received news that Gulf Air planned their first 'trial' flight that very day, and that we should get the first planeload of passengers down to Abadan as soon as possible. The wardens had already told those on the first flight to be ready to leave at any time at one hour's notice. So I immediately went and told Tom Evans and Mike Hall, and they in turn notified the wardens and also our aircraft crews that flights to Abadan should begin as soon as possible. As I had no operational phone at home, I could not let Ginny or Sue (who were both on the first flight out) know, but Cliff promised to go round and see them immediately.

I had also been told by IROS that if the flight on the 29th was successful, Gulf Air planned on two or more flights per day thereafter, so the team started to put together two further flight manifests for me to deal with. The news that the evacuation was on spread like wildfire among the expat community. We had some 1,300 people to get out, so it was going to take some time.

On 30 December we received a telex from Athens, relayed via IROS, that the first real evacuation flight had landed at Athens at 11.45 p.m. local time, giving us the manifest of those who had arrived. I was so glad to see that my wife, Sue Wedlake and my good friend Otto Selis (whose wife we had previously got out with their cats) were on that list. Apparently the three of them were filmed by the BBC coming down the steps of the aircraft as the first evacuees (App. 9).

I have asked Ginny to write the next chapter with her experience of how she got out. I, of course, was not even able to say goodbye to her, and had no idea how her journey and the first trial flight out had gone.

The following morning all military protection was withdrawn on the orders of a mullah sent in by Khomeini, and our guard just handed me the keys of the house and said he had been ordered to leave. John Raoofi, whom I had told about the cats incident, advised against my going back to the house and so, as New Year approached, I became a bit of a nomad, sleeping at the houses of other expats. We had an Iranian couple staying next door to us, and sadly I had to pass Dimple and Haig over the wall to them to look after. We never saw, or heard of, those two delightful animals again.

Ginny's Story

For the days after Paul Grimm's assassination when James had been spending up to fifteen hours a day organising our eventual evacuation, Dimple and Haig were my very alert guards. It was as if they knew that things were not right, and they hardly left the house – when they did it was only into the confines of the garden. They would always be in the house by dusk and as our electricity supply was somewhat spasmodic by then, I would sit in our sitting room, mostly in the dark with the two cats either on my lap or nearby, waiting for James to arrive home safely. The cats were the first to be alerted at the slightest noise outside and it was amazing how very sensitive they were.

Each residential area in Ahwaz had elected an expatriate warden whose responsibility it was to make sure that all expatriates in his area knew of any changes in curfew times, and eventually to coordinate the evacuation of his charges. Cliff Lucas was our area warden. We had been told to have two suitcases packed and ready to go at short notice, and as there were unlikely to be any baggage handlers at the airport, no more than we could carry ourselves.

Trying to decide what to pack from our life of nearly five years in Iran was a most difficult task. We had been accumulating beautiful Persian rugs, local copper, glass and silverware, most of which was far too heavy or fragile to contemplate packing. However, I did manage to put one particularly fine rug in the bottom of one suitcase with a copper plate and bowl wrapped inside. Otherwise, I packed all the family photographs of the girls growing up, as I felt that they were of sentimental value and quite irreplaceable. I packed very few clothes, being of the view that I needed just a couple of changes of clothing; otherwise everything was replaceable. I had intimated to James that, should he have time, there were a few favourite clothes that I would like him to bring for me. Sadly we had to leave all our books, paintings etc. One thing I have always regretted not packing was a loose-leaf book of recipes I had collected throughout the years from various countries where I had lived.

On the day of our evacuation, Sue Wedlake arrived at the house, as she and Graham were intending to move in with us until we were evacuated. I had awoken that morning to find that, unusually, we had both power and water, so Sue and I both took the opportunity to wash our hair. At about 8 a.m., when we were about to dry our hair, Cliff came to the house to tell us that our area, Kien Pars, was to be evacuated first, as it was nearest to the bazaar area and therefore more vulnerable. We were to be ready to go to the airport in ten minutes' time! So all thoughts of drying our hair were put aside, and we just had time to grab a quiche from the freezer and close our bags before Cliff drove us to the airport. Of course I had no way of letting James know that we had gone and, more importantly, no idea if I would ever see him again.

The sergeant was back guarding the house that day, and he helped load our luggage into Cliff's car. His rifle kept slipping off his shoulder, so he gave it to me to hold!

When Sue and I arrived at Ahwaz Airport, we found that landing rights for Gulf Air in Abadan had still not been obtained. We were being ferried down to Abadan in small Twin Otter aircraft – these were OSCO aircraft, which the expatriate pilots had volunteered to fly. We first had a two-hour wait at Ahwaz Airport but finally took off. As we flew over Ahwaz we could still see smoke coming from several buildings – eight banks had been burnt down. At Abadan we had another wait of about seven hours. Since leaving the house we had been given nothing to eat or drink, so eventually we decided to eat the quiche… having thawed in a plastic bag and not having been heated in the oven, it was rather revoltingly soggy! But it was better than nothing. That was all we had until about 9 p.m. that evening – nothing whatsoever to drink all that day.

Gulf Air ferried us to Bahrain in 737s and then from Bahrain to Athens in TriStars – 'the Gulf Air five-star TriStar', as it came to be known. I have flown many airlines in my life, but never, ever, have any of us had the superb treatment Gulf Air gave us. The first Gulf Air flight to come into Abadan, the one on which Sue and I were flown out, came in still with no landing rights or runway lights. The crew themselves did all the baggage handling – all the crews were expatriate. The very second the wheels left the tarmac when we took off, all the passengers spontaneously cheered and clapped. Less than a minute later, we were all given whatever we wanted to drink, courtesy of Gulf Air. Then, when we took off from Bahrain for Athens, dinner was served, with wine, courtesy of Gulf Air. Dinner, by any standards, but especially after a day of abstinence, was simply superb. We were all given as many helpings as we could eat. This was of course long before the days of the plastic packaged airline meals with which we are all now too familiar.

We arrived in Athens shortly after 1.30 a.m. Ahwaz time, so it had been a long day. On arrival at our hotel, we were both too keyed up for sleep, so we sat up talking in the bar (with one or two local brandies!) for quite some time before going to bed. We were sharing a room. After only a few hours' sleep, there was a knock at our bedroom door and a voice saying, 'Mrs Lawson – I understand you can type and that you would be willing to help out in the office.'

This had been set up in the basement of the hotel to handle the operation. James had apparently told the London office of IROS in one of his telexes that I would be happy to help out. The office was vastly understaffed, BP/IROS having sent out just one secretary and four men to coordinate the entire operation. I was given the job of running the office and getting everything organised – at that time we did not even have any typewriters, just telex machines. Sue and another of the wives from the Contracts Department came in to help out the following day, and the three of us, for the next week or so, worked up to fifteen hours a day.

These were perhaps the hardest and longest hours I have ever worked; we didn't even stop for lunch, but had sandwiches and beer brought in for us. But certainly it was the most rewarding and exciting work. It also kept us all mentally occupied, so that we hardly had time to worry about our husbands, all of whom were still in Ahwaz. I found myself back on the telex machine, and although I couldn't speak directly to James (who, from the previous Friday until the day he left Ahwaz, did nothing but operate the telex machine, organising the evacuation from the Ahwaz end), I was at least indirectly in contact with him through the London office, so at least knew he was still safe.

The hotel we were booked into in Athens was first class, the Apollon Palace Hotel. It was beautifully situated on the beach – although it took us about three days before we actually found that out, as we never had time to go out of the hotel! The passengers off the first two planes were put in our hotel, and we subsequently took over three more hotels. It was an almost impossible task trying to locate exactly what members of which family had arrived and in which hotel they were so that IROS could be informed, in order to notify the next of kin. We had the manifest of the passengers of each planeload telexed to us, and it was our responsibility to try to get male members of family into the same hotel as their wives who had already arrived in Athens. This was particularly difficult when all we had was a surname; so if, for instance, the name was Smith, of which there were several in OSCO, we were not sure to which Mrs Smith he belonged!

New Year's Eve came and went – it was just another day in the office! However, the following day I managed to get a call through to James in Ahwaz. He was no longer living in our house. The day after I had left, all military protection had been withdrawn, so our house guard had just handed back the keys and announced that he was returning to his unit. Khomeini had apparently sent in a mullah, who had appointed a Strike Committee of five, and they had stipulated that the military were to withdraw from all homes and the office.

On the evening of 4 January I tried to call James again. I had a message from some friends in London about someone still in Ahwaz with a visa problem, so I was trying to inform James so that it would be sorted out, in order that they could be evacuated. I knew from telexes from London that James was staying with Jimmy Paton. The line, when I finally got through, was extremely bad. I heard Jimmy saying that James was out, and as I knew it was after curfew, I could not understand this. It took me some while to realise that he was telling me that James was out of Iran and that he should be with me the following day.

As luck would have it, our telex in the Athens office

broke down (with all the overwork, no doubt!) the following afternoon. We therefore received no manifest of passengers due in at Athens that evening. I did not dare to go to the airport in case James did not arrive, but had a friend going there who would bring him to the hotel if he was there. When James walked into the office I had just got London on the line (the telex was now working) with some very urgent queries, so I didn't know whether to abandon the telex or James!

James was, of course, bombarded with questions all that evening, not only from us in the office, but from all the other wives whose husbands were still in Ahwaz. James had been operating the telex all that week, and on the morning of the day he left, one of the senior Iranian managers had received a phone call from one of the strike leaders saying that it was known who was operating the telex, and that James was to be given fifteen minutes to get out of the office and fifteen minutes to get home, pack and get to the airport – or they would not be answerable for what happened to him.

So he was ordered to leave. We later learnt that James's name had been seen written in Farsi in one of the mosques as the next target, i.e. top of the hit list. James rushed home and literally grabbed the first things he found and bundled them into a suitcase – he left so quickly that the Christmas decorations were all still up, the tree still standing with its fairy lights, and there were over one hundred mince pies in the freezer that I had baked for the New Year's Day party we were to have given...

In James's haste to pack he had remembered that there were a few favourite clothes that I wanted him to bring. At the expense of his kilt, kilt jacket etc., he had gallantly packed what he thought I would like. Unfortunately, he arrived in Athens with all the clothes that I had said I would be delighted to never see again, and had left behind those that I would have liked! But so what? He was back with me, safe and sound; and in just five days 1,300 people, mostly British or American, had been safely evacuated.

Athens

I had no idea, of course, whether Ginny had got out or not, as I was cooped up in the telex room occupied with the next day's flight. However, I had sent one of my most reliable expats, Mike Hogg, out to Ahwaz Airport to monitor and supervise the flights in the F27s and Twin Otters from Ahwaz to Abadan. Later that afternoon Mike tapped on my door and told me the flights had departed Ahwaz, albeit later than planned because of obstructive air traffic control permission. This was to become a persistent problem that we had to deal with for both Ahwaz and Abadan.

We had had to send down one of my expat computer staff to Abadan with a fair amount of hastily gathered rials from departing evacuees to 'smooth' the required clearance and consents. As it turned out, he was absolutely brilliant, and for a little man, whom you would have thought wouldn't say 'boo' to a goose, he set himself up behind one of the check-in desks at Abadan Airport, completely abandoned by then, found some boarding passes, and with a copy of my passenger manifest checked passengers' identities and issued them with boarding passes; it is to my great regret that I cannot remember his name – but he did an outstanding job.

That same day, Bagher Mohammadi, the General Manager of Engineering and Construction, with whom I had worked very closely, just disappeared with his wife and family, and we later learnt that he had been arrested and detained at Tehran's Mehrabad Airport. Bagher and I had negotiated several very major contracts, some over $600 million in value with major American, Dutch and British international contractors. Apparently it was felt that Bagher was 'in the pockets' of some of these contractors, and so was a much wanted man by the revolutionaries. We think that it was he who had told the Iranian contractor in Tehran about the attempt on my life (they were very close friends and had been at university together), and hence the phone call to me from that man re the cats saving our lives.

It was a very long day at the office and I was extremely tired; as I left the office I saw that my car had been broken into, a window smashed and a tyre slashed; it was about the last straw. It was pitch dark and there was no light. An office guard, still loyal, came over and gave me a hand to change the tyre, holding lighted matches until his fingers burned so that I could see the wheel nuts.

Back in the office in the morning I learnt from IROS that all the first set of evacuees were now in a hotel in Athens and were well and safe. I had advised IROS the day before that when Ginny and Sue arrived, if they were pushed, they had two top-class secretaries available, Ginny having been, as I have said, a secretary in U Thant's office in New York, when he was Secretary General of the United Nations.

By this time, I had become pretty expert in telex operation, and IROS had taught me to pre-cut tapes of passenger manifests so that I could run them through, as and when we were informed of further flights by Gulf Air. IROS, in turn, ran them through to the hotel in Athens, so that they knew whom to expect and when and arrange accommodation for them or, later, for them to rejoin their wives. So I sort of tacked on a message each day for them to relay to Ginny (as I knew she would have been roped in to the office) that I was safe.

The flights out from Ahwaz from 30 December onwards were increasingly difficult to control. Once people knew that flights were running and evacuation on the way, many other non-OSCO expats, drillers, contractors, engineers etc., rushed to the airport demanding to be put on planes and, regrettably, some even tried to haul women off the aircraft steps, including six-foot drillers who should have known better. Mike Hogg and his boys did an excellent job in dealing with the situation.

One of the few benefits of remaining while people left was that we were inundated with gifts, from those on their way out, of both food and surplus alcohol. We had really got things under way now, and it became pretty frantic for me to keep everyone informed with the news coming in from IROS. The PAX microwave linking with the OSCO and Shell offices in Tehran was thankfully still working, so that we could coordinate getting some people out to Abadan from Tehran and then fly them on to Athens.

There were no commercial flights out of Tehran, and landing permits were almost impossible to obtain for the OSCO F27s (App. 10). An attempt to get a Gulf Air 737 straight into Mehrabad Airport proved impossible – a great pity, as it could have taken all expatriates and their families on the one flight. One could only admire the dogged persistence of Captain Cameron and his pilots in just going ahead anyway to extricate these people and take them to Abadan for onward travel to Athens. He kindly flew up from Abadan to Ahwaz with my warfarin tablets and, as I said in my telex to London (App. 11), 'bang goes my last excuse for leaving'!

Our helicopters were also busy bringing in people from remote operating plants or construction sites. Again, it was another long day – but I did immensely appreciate the support given to me by Tom Evans and John Raoofi. I can't remember exactly where I slept that night, but I do remember sampling some of the finer malt whiskies left behind.

On 31 December (Hogmanay) more flights went out as per the manifest, with yet more money having to be scraped up to grease palms. Jimmy Paton (at the so-called 'Scottish Embassy') had invited Graham Wedlake and me to stay with him. Jimmy was a great 'fixer' of visas, or work permits or whatever was needed; as a lawyer and notary public, I had frequently been working with him on people's personal needs and problems. As we came to his house, pretty tired after another long day, Jimmy announced that we were jolly well going to have a party and bring in the New Year properly in great style. His bar was awash with booze donated from evacuees, and Christine, his wife, and their cook had pulled out all the stops to produce a most excellent meal for us, liberally washed down with the best wines.

As the evening progressed, the assembled company got noisier and noisier – a sort of pent-up temporary relief – and on came the Scottish dance music. After dinner we settled into the serious business of addressing all the malt whisky on the bar, and I am afraid we all ended up a little the worse for wear. I remember a game of darts was attempted, but by that time our aim was somewhat 'blurred', and we had to get the houseboys to throw the darts while we pointed out on the dartboard which number we wanted them to hit! We also had an interruption, when we realised that some Iranians were on the roof of the building, some of them armed and shouting loudly. Somehow, Jimmy persuaded them to leave by sending his houseboy out with some cash, which seemed to solve the problem.

The first day of January 1979 was just another spent at the telex, with more flights going out, and more non-OSCO expats arriving and pleading to be evacuated; I remember some French from the sugar plantation further north, who arrived absolutely desperate, having had a terrible time and their lives threatened. As Total, the French oil company, was by then my parent company, I felt an obligation towards them, and Tom Evans agreed that we should help them as space and seats permitted. We had more trouble at Ahwaz Airport that day, as a seismic team just arrived and abandoned their vehicles at the airport, still packed with explosives, and demanded to be flown out. It was another long and difficult day. That evening was quieter than Hogmanay, but we again had people on the roof at the Scottish Embassy, which was pretty disquieting. However, I was very grateful for Jimmy and Christine's hospitality, and I had been able to speak to Ginny, as their phone, for some reason, was still operative.

During the odd conversation that I was able to have from either Cliff Lucas or Dr Crawford's house with Jim Porter, he stressed the concern of the member companies, who considered it was essential that an expatriate presence was kept on after the main body of evacuees had left. We were asked to find about sixty volunteers prepared to take the risk, as that was felt to be the minimum amount that NIOC would accept as OSCO not having violated the terms of its contract with NIOC securing production rights to the oil majors. As I remember, Tom Evans put that list together, and I typed it up and telexed it out on 1 January. I was asked the following day by Jim Porter to confirm the details of the 'band of volunteers' (App. 12) and I noticed that Tom had just put my name on the list as staying on! Mike Hogg and Jerry Gilbert, who figure later in this book, were also volunteers (App. 12).

On the morning of 4 January I was in the office early as

usual, setting to with the next passenger manifest and receiving information on planned flights and times from IROS, when John Raoofi knocked on the door of the telex cubbyhole and asked me to come out and talk to him. John told me that I had to leave at once, as I was no longer safe. We both went into Tom Evans' office and I stated that I was sure that I would be all right. However, John then said that the revolutionaries knew that I was operating the telex as a 'strike-breaker' and helping to organise the evacuation, and both he and Tom insisted that they did not want another Paul Grimm, and that it would be better for all if I left immediately. I was told that I should be out of the office in no more than ten minutes, as my safety was at risk. I did a very hurried short instruction course to one of Mike Hall's staff as to how to operate the telex, and told IROS they would have a new communicator. I then went to my office to pick up a few things, and was driven to our house to pack one bag. That was when, in my panic, I gallantly forewent my kilt and kilt evening dress and grabbed one set of clothes on a divided rail in Ginny's wardrobe and stuffed them in my holdall.

I was driven straight to Ahwaz Airport, where an Alouette helicopter was waiting for me, said goodbye to Mike Hogg, and was flown down to Abadan in time to join the Gulf Air flight out that day.

As an aside, we had twenty-six helicopters from a Dutch company, and as I remember, after the Revolution, they were 'spirited' out of Iran. This was the subject of a fascinating book entitled *Whirlwind*.

When we arrived in Bahrain, while waiting to board the TriStar on to Athens, one of the consular staff came to speak with me. He wished to know details of just how bad things were in Ahwaz, and what we knew of other expats still left there. I had to tell him that I thought that one could not believe other than that the Revolution was inevitable and the Shah would certainly be deposed. I told him that the sooner this was recognised and accepted by the Foreign Office, and plans made accordingly, the better.

I also had time to call Jim Porter from the airport at Bahrain, before boarding the TriStar to Athens (App. 13). I knew that several expatriate contractors on some of the construction projects were having difficulty in being 'pulled out', as they did not have the same contacts to get rescue flights authorised; they had no equivalent of a John Raoofi. I felt very strongly that, as we had brought them over to work on our projects in the first place, we could not just abandon them, get ourselves out and then just leave them unassisted. It was very gratifying, later, to see the passenger manifests with the French from the sugar plantation and many contractor personnel included, as having been flown out courtesy of OSCO/IROS.

We were absolutely superbly looked after by Gulf Air cabin crew, both on the flight from Abadan to Bahrain and again on from there to Athens. It is a sad reflection as to how the standard of airline food has slipped so appallingly since those great days of flying. Gulf Air will for ever be, and remain, in my and Ginny's minds the best airline in the world, and we are so grateful for the superb and professional job done by their pilots and crew.

I was disappointed, on arrival in Athens, not to find Ginny at the airport to meet me, but she had asked one of the BP staff flown over from London, who was handling people arriving off the flight and telling them what hotel they were booked into, to look out for me. He kindly took me to the main hotel and told me how very hard she and Sue had been working, and that Ginny was still in the office.

Going into the large room taken over by the staff as the hub of the Athens end of the evacuation was a really emotional experience. Ginny looked up from the telex machine she was sitting at, saw me and then rushed over, and we were in each other's arms, realising just how much we loved each other and how wonderful it was to be reunited. I went up to our room – poor old Sue had to decamp and move to another room – where I had a most blissful bath, with glass in hand.

Ginny came in some time later, and I told her how suddenly I'd had to leave because of the threat to my life. I proudly showed her the clothes I had brought back for her at the expense of my kilt, and her face dropped – to confirm that I had brought out the clothes she did not care about – not the ones she really wanted! However, nothing seemed to matter now that we were back together again.

We went down to the bar for a drink before dinner, and all those expats already out, mostly wives, rushed over to find out if I had any news… had I seen their husbands, and how bad things were out there. This continued well into the night after dinner, and we were both pretty exhausted when we went to bed. The following morning Ginny was back on duty, and after breakfast I was asked to go into the office for a consultation on the situation. I spoke at length with Jim Porter in London and with George Link, who, as I remember, had flown over from the States to be in the IROS office.

The main topic of discussion was what to do next. There was obviously a strong desire from member companies to maintain a hold over these most valuable of assets in Iran, producing up to 5 million barrels a day of high-grade crude oil (when all was well). This was reinforced by the views of some that perhaps there had been an overreaction in evacuating personnel, when the American and UK Governments were still maintaining that the Shah's regime would restore order, that the Revolution would be crushed and would not result in Ayatollah Khomeini returning to Iran to claim power.

I could only advise them that, from what we had seen on the ground, the fall of the Shah was inevitable, and the sooner the member companies recognised that the better. The army had by this time almost totally deserted, as we had witnessed in Ahwaz, while in Tehran the rioting, burning of buildings, murder and arrests of those loyal to the Shah were getting worse by the day. Despite that, at that time, it was still felt by the oil majors that all OSCO personnel should be kept together, and that things might calm down and we could all return, take back control of the oilfields, reoccupy our office and houses, and that things would gradually revert to normal – as it had been before the Revolution began to grow momentum. This was not a view that I shared, but there was some desperation at the thought of the losses that would result and the impact on the oil price, as availability of Iranian crude reduced to virtually zero; these were high stakes.

It was recognised that evacuees and their families staying in Athens for any great length of time, spread out over three hotels, was difficult to sustain. Many Americans and British expats just wanted to go home, see their parents and relatives, and have some leave while the situation in Iran unfolded and the vision of the future there became clearer and was determined. You just had to have lived through it to see and understand the fanaticism of the Islamic feeling, the demonstrated willingness of people ready to 'die for Allah', and the grass roots uprising throughout the whole of Iran to go back to an Islamic way of life ruled by the mullahs. To those of us who lived through it, it was obvious that the Shah's time was over.

If one looks at the history of Iran, it can be seen that the regime of the shahs was imposed upon Iran after the end of the Second World War by the Allied Powers. The Shah, on the plus side, was clearly trying to modernise Iran and move it forward two centuries in a short space of time. He had built up the world's fourth most powerful army, brought in American and British forces to train up the Iranian military and air force, and while he had many good goals and ideals, he had operated a brutal and harsh regime, which was to be his downfall.

Sending personnel back to America and the UK was also going to have major tax implications for expatriate personnel, as all enjoyed a tax-free status in Iran and were classified as non-residents in their own country. Consequently, they could only visit their home country for a limited space of time before becoming liable to tax on their incomes. As the representative in Iran of Total, the French oil company, I was not at all sure what would happen to me in the future.

It was decided that OSCO should try to 'regroup' in a tax-free location, set up a holding office there, and move evacuees to that country and then let them visit their own countries on leave within an allowed time frame that did not contravene their tax-free status. As Bahrain and Gulf Air had been so stunningly helpful in getting us to safety, George asked me to go back there the next day and explore what options there were in that country. I took my lawyer, Graham Wedlake, with me and Jim Cushing, the Drilling Manager – as we had rigs to rescue from offshore. It was felt that Bahrain was conveniently close to Iran, should we ever be in a position to go back.

The incoming Gulf Air TriStar had stayed overnight at

Athens Airport and was headed back early in the morning in time to turn around in Bahrain and bring the next load of evacuees out later that day. So the three of us had a very memorable flight back in the first-class cabin, with a full crew and just us. Champagne was provided before take-off, and then an excellent breakfast, with cocktails before we landed. As usual, the first-class attention from the cabin crew could not be faulted, and it was most interesting to have time to sit and talk to them. The captain also came back for a chat, and when he learnt that I was a pilot, he invited me to the cockpit to sit in the jump seat for the final approach and landing into Bahrain; I think that without doubt, apart from flying on Concorde on four occasions, it was the most memorable flight ever!

When we had landed, Gulf Air whisked us through Customs and we were driven to meet the Commercial Attaché at the British Consular Office, and then to meet a top Bahraini lawyer, who briefed us on how to set up 'OSCO Bahrain' and go through the formalities that would be required, as we would have to have a local 'sponsor', which we were assured would be no problem. In addition, we were informed that OSCO employees would have a tax-free status. The whole premise was based upon keeping the organisation together, so that if the Shah did prevail, we could go back and resume operations as before. I was not, however, in any way sanguine about this being a possibility. We were told that OSCO would be made most welcome.

We joined the returning flight to Athens late that after-noon with the next outgoing evacuees, who were somewhat surprised to see us on-board, and again bombarded us with questions as to what would happen to them when they got to Athens, and what accommodation they were going to find. I was able to assure them that by that time BP/IROS had taken over no less than three top-class hotels, and that if their wives were already out they would be sent to join them and that they would want for nothing. As I remember, a pretty generous per diem allowance had been set up, over and above the hotel costs so that, arriving with very little, they could go out and buy toiletries and clothes etc. In those days, Athens was the place to buy fur coats, and many of the ladies took full advantage of that!

The following morning I was back in the office talking to Jim Porter in IROS with a full report on how the trip to Bahrain had gone, and what the possibilities were there. During that conversation I was told that George Link thought that I would be more useful back in London; the evacuation was in its final stages, going well, and more support staff had been sent out to Athens from London, so Ginny could also stand down from working such long hours in the office.

Back in London

We flew out on our own the following morning on a BA flight to Heathrow and got a taxi from there and reopened our house in Teddington. We had also kept a car there. Opening the door to the house was very strange and in a way lonely experience. We had left behind so many great friends and colleagues in Athens, with whom we had been through so much, with no knowledge of what was going to happen to them all; however, at least we knew that they were now safe.

It was even more of a strange feeling to get up the following morning, put on a suit and start walking to Teddington station, with all the other commuters, to take the train up to London. Ginny was going straight off to see her father in Harrow, so she needed the car. On arrival at the IROS office in Finsbury Square, it was an emotional experience to meet Jim Porter again, with such great working friends as Peter Marshall, Fred Williamson, Ken Snooks and many others. I was taken into a meeting room thereafter, with a whole host of personnel and other staff who wanted a full account of events and the situation in Iran as we had left it.

There seemed to be some concern as to whether we really did need to pull everybody out, or whether it would be possible to keep thirty to forty people out there as a kind of skeleton staff, as it were, because of the immense value of the investment there, the consequences relative to oil production and the contract with NIOC. I had to say that, in my view, the way things were going in Iran it was unsafe to leave any expatriate to the mercy of the Islamic fanaticism that we had witnessed; they could see for themselves from television reports from Tehran that Iran was a country in complete anarchy.

Just before lunch, Jim took me downstairs to the big telex room where the Communications Manager and all the telex and telephone staff were gathered together, and as soon as I walked into the room, they all stood up and burst into applause. Then I heard a champagne cork pop (this was in the days before 'alcohol-free' offices!) and we all had a glass or two.

As we were celebrating, there was a call for silence and the manager came over and presented me with a parchment scroll tied in a red ribbon, which he invited me to read. It said:

THIS IS TO CERTIFY
THAT

JAMES LAWSON

HAVING BEEN DULY TRAINED AND INSTRUCTED BY
THE COMMUNICATIONS TEAM AT IROS
HAS NOW QUALIFIED
AS A TELEX OPERATOR – GRADE 2

I was extremely touched and humbled by that presentation, but rather upset that I had only passed as 'Grade 2'!

The following day I was invited to join a meeting of all the oil company shareholders' representatives, BP, Shell, Exxon, Texaco, Total etc., and the IROS senior management. It was a large meeting and all were anxious to have a first-hand report on the situation in Iran and how things were going with the evacuation. I gave them the best report I could. The discussion then moved on to 'Where do we go from here?' There were still divided views as to whether the Shah's downfall was inevitable, or whether there was a possibility that matters would result in the uprising being quashed and OSCO personnel being able to return to reclaim the priceless oilfields. I seem to remember that a decision was reached that one should try to 'hang on' and keep the staff together in case a return was possible.

I was pretty astonished at the lunch that followed the meeting (which seemed to be a customary monthly ritual). Not only was the food excellent, but the wine flowed freely, and at the end of the meal port and cigars were made available and I could see members taking about three or four Romeo & Julieta cigars, lighting one and putting the rest in their pockets... how the other half lived!

The question of what to do with all the Athens evacuees was still a problem; the evacuation process was all but finalised and there were three hotels full of expats wondering what was to be their future. While Bahrain was still an option, feelings crept in that it was too far from the UK and the USA; and as the situation worsened, confidence in the survival of the Shah and the return of OSCO personnel to Iran were diminishing. The tax problem, however, still loomed large and a 'tax haven' closer to home was sought. So I was sent down to Jersey, with Ginny, to look at the options there, Ginny coming to assess how wives and children would take to life in the Channel Islands, what schools were available etc.

We were very warmly received by the hotel staff, who seemed to be aware of the purpose of our visit, and were given absolutely top-class service and even given the superb 'honeymoon suite'! I had meetings with the Jersey offices of one of the major London law firms whom BP used, and we went through the required details of setting up OSCO (CI) Ltd, and also what would be the tax treatment of OSCO personnel coming to live there on a temporary basis of three to six months. While it was work, it was a lovely break for us to be in the better climate of the Channel Islands, and to sit and have dinner together in the evening and to relax a little after all that we had been through.

Back in London afterwards, I wrote up a report to be circulated to the OSCO oil company members, which had either Bahrain or Jersey as possibilities. However, as the days went by and the situation in Iran steadily worsened, the prospects of keeping the OSCO staff together became more and more remote.

The first decision taken, as I remember it, was to terminate the employment of the direct hire personnel and bring them back from Athens to their location of hire. As it was unlikely that they would ever see the contents of their homes in Iran again, each was asked to complete an inventory and valuation estimate of their personal possessions and furniture, cars etc. that they had left behind. As far as I am aware, as the uprising in Iran was an act of war, riot or rebellion, there was no insurance cover, so it was the consortium of oil companies who were to foot the bill. Part of my job, in London, then became going over the submitted inventories and the values put upon the items left behind. Having known and visited many of the homes in question, I can only comment that I rarely came across anything that had been undervalued!

The Gulf Air evacuation flights had, by this time, come to an end. However a few stalwarts had volunteered to stay behind to at least keep a token OSCO presence. There follows just a sample personal account of three of the men who were prepared to stay on but who found it impossible. The last man out was Jerry Gilbert; I had forgotten that he had been taken to hospital in Abadan with hepatitis, and the story of his escape is recorded in a most excellent Pulitzer Prize-winning book, *The Prize – The Epic Quest for Oil, Money and Power*, by Daniel Yergin, which covers the history of the oil industry, makes fascinating reading and includes an account of the Iranian Revolution. It also refers to the expatriate evacuation, which has been the subject of this book; I would recommend it as well worth reading.

On 16 January 1979, the end finally came, and the Shah left Iran and flew to Egypt with a casket of Iranian soil in his luggage; he was never to return again. The crowds went wild with jubilation, statues were ripped down, portraits smashed and felled and the country seemed rudderless – all awaiting the return of Khomeini. He flew in from Paris on 1 February that year and received a rapturous welcome at Mehrabad Airport. We knew then that this was the end of OSCO. However, by that time, apart from the very sad death of Paul Grimm, all OSCO personnel were out of Iran and we had rescued many other expatriates besides our own staff.

Anthony ('Tony') Gilbert

Tony arrived to join the contract staff of OSCO's Tehran office in 1974, reporting to my Head of Contracts there, Hassan Mohebbi. A bachelor, Tony very quickly settled into life in the office, established a good working relationship with Hassan, and became an excellent member of staff. He also thought that Tehran was the best posting in the Middle East – 'especially as a bachelor, like myself'. He enjoyed a lively social life, visiting the excellent restaurants, theatre and cinemas with expatriate friends quickly made. His love of skiing was fulfilled, as in the winter the 'Shah' sport was well organised up in the mountains to the north of Tehran, and it was his intention to stay in Iran for a considerable length of time. This is his story.

I was thoroughly enjoying my life in Tehran both at work and socially since my arrival, seconded from BP in 1974, until 1977 when the signs of unrest had become apparent. This appears to have been triggered by the views expressed by Jimmy Carter, the US President, relative to his seeing fit to interfere with what I believe were his exaggerated accounts of how the Shah ran his country. He made 'human rights' demands without really understanding the situation in Iran that the Shah had to 'juggle' with. The Shah, under pressure, agreed to allow, for the first time, freedom to demonstrate, freedom of the press etc., as a prelude to promised free elections the following year.

Excessive advantage was immediately taken of this

unaccustomed taste of freedom and pressure built up with frightening rapidity. The people, given an inch, tried to take a mile, and in the first week of September 1978 (only a few days after their first taste of freedom to demonstrate) there was a huge procession of over 250,000 people carrying banners through Tehran. They were actually peaceful, but when they started shouting against the Shah, he had second thoughts and demonstrations were forbidden. The people ignored this and staged another one on 8 September – but the army were waiting for them, not only with rifles, but with heavy machine guns. They were, again, peaceful but they refused to disperse when ordered to do so and the army opened fire.

This was reported in England as '120 killed' by troops in Tehran. In fact, there were about 3,000 killed, half being women and children – pure murder, as the troops kept firing at people trying to run away. Down in the bazaar area, near OSCO's offices where it happened, you had only to see the number of people wearing black to realise the extent of the carnage. This did not exactly increase the Shah's popularity, and it is significant that all the other members of the Royal Family (except Queen Farah, who stood by him) were out of the country and did not return after 'Black Friday', as it quickly became known.

The British reporter for the *Guardian* newspaper was thrown out of Iran at the end of September after trying to get into the cemetery in Tehran, where the bodies were buried, to count the graves. The Shah made an unprece-dented appearance on television to try to restore his authority to what it had been only a few weeks earlier, but it was already too late. Khomeini and his supporters were able to establish a strong platform, despite the Shah controlling what were then the fourth largest armed forces in the world.

Shortly after these events, martial law was declared and a curfew imposed extending from midnight to 4.30 a.m. Anybody found outside during curfew hours was liable to be shot on sight – and this was ruthlessly enforced. Social life was quickly structured around curfew hours and I commented in my letters home that 'it now seems so normal that one would think that it had always been so'.

As the weeks passed, life and even ordinary conversation soon became difficult, as Iranians' views polarised, with the religious extremists quickly frightening the majority to the point where they were wary of expressing their true political views, even to friends – especially any words of support for the Shah's regime. In Tehran's OSCO office, many of the obligatory pictures of the Royal Family on office walls quietly disappeared. On questioning this, I was told that they were being cleaned! At the same time, the army became very active on the streets, as violence increased, and large armed patrols and military convoys were to be seen every day.

In October the Shah was still strongly entrenched and the army officers were absolutely loyal to him, but security was increasing day by day. From late October, through November, mobs roamed the streets during the day, but always retreated when the army appeared. We saw, from our office windows several floors up, many acts of violence, including the trashing and firebombing of our own branch of Bank Etebarate on the ground floor of the same block. We also saw the looting and total destruction of a liquor store, with the pleading owner being beaten senseless on the pavement – quite awful. As soon as the army appeared (never from far away) the mob miraculously evaporated.

But the army were quite aggressive too. One day I remember a lot of shooting outside and went round to the office of a colleague, Mansour Alavi, which had the best view of the boulevard below. We saw about one hundred soldiers walking slowly down the street in line abreast, filling the entire width of the road and pavements; they were firing blanks into the air. I was leaning out of the window watching all this when a soldier took exception to me and waved his gun, indicating to me to 'get back inside'.

I knew that they only had blanks, as they were having to cock the gun after each round, so I just shook my head. This chap then ostentatiously removed his magazine from his rifle and replaced it with another. I dived back and he fired, the bullet passing right through the metal window frame without breaking the glass. However, we generally felt quite safe inside the office, as I think it had some priority protection from the army, and apart from that incident, they never bothered us.

OSCO's Tehran office was in the south of the city, but most of the expats lived way up in the northern suburbs, necessitating a long drive every day down to the office. No thought was given to closing the office; work obviously had to go on. We, the expats, were easily recognisable in the streets, being plainly not of Middle Eastern appearance. We were frequently accused loudly of being Americans, who were by now seen as 'Satans' by the zealots.

As life became more difficult, we were told to take a different route to work every day and vary our times of leaving and returning. One day, driving back from the office (alone), I turned a corner to find a large mob of shrieking Iranians blocking the street. My car was quickly surrounded and the mob tried to turn it over with me (locked) inside. My previous rally driving hobby came to my rescue and I did the craziest high-speed reversing, knocking several of them aside; I then spun the car and raced away. On another occasion, I was buying groceries in the Kourosh super-market, with lots of people around, when a bearded man came over and said, 'Not for you, Emirikai!' and proceeded to throw everything in my trolley on the ground; needless to say, I did not wait to pick it all up!

By now the curfew hours had been increased and started from 9 p.m. This was heavily enforced by the army and police, and thousands of them were on the streets armed with automatic rifles and empowered (and also willing, as frequently demonstrated) to shoot to kill without any warning. Also, from early November the two English language newspapers ceased to appear, and the TV was so heavily censored it was laughable.

There was now no way of enjoying a meal out at a restaurant, theatre or cinema (most of these having been burnt down anyway). The 'situation' boringly became many people's sole topic of conversation; even my French classes, which accounted for three good social evenings a week, were cancelled indefinitely. Living alone, I spent long evenings playing backgammon against myself with a computer, and with its help became very good and spent much time studying the mathematics of world champions' moves!

At this time, I was still, optimistically, looking forward to the start of skiing up at Dizin, and in one letter home I refused a suggestion that I go back to the UK for Christmas 1978 and said, 'Just one more snowfall and we're away.' As the security situation seemed to have stabilised a bit, and flights into Tehran had resumed, I invited my girlfriend in England to come out and spend Christmas in Tehran, much against the wishes of her parents; the television in the UK had made Tehran look like Beirut at its worst. I knew that we would have to behave sensibly and keep a low profile.

She agreed to come out, and her Pan Am flight arrived before curfew at 7.30 p.m. so there were no dramas. However, skiing was out so we remained cooped up in the flat for ten days. Although I had to disappear to the office on normal working days, we enjoyed a fantastic Christmas, with all the trimmings brought over from England, isolating ourselves from everything outside. On 30 December, my girlfriend got what turned out to be one of the last scheduled flights out of Mehrabad, as the situation worsened again. The plane was delayed for several hours while the pilot bargained for fuel with the military, who eventually only supplied enough fuel to get to Istanbul, where they had to land for more.

Back on my own, after dark there was non-stop gunfire echoing round the city all night, sometimes machine guns too, and occasionally the 'boom' of tanks firing their big guns. After 9 p.m. I, like most people, went up to the flat roof to enjoy the fresh air. It was eerie; there was this huge city, spread out below, with a backdrop of the Elburz Mountains, but absolutely deserted streets and boulevards. Not a person or vehicle was moving, apart from the occasional long convoys of military lorries driving round slowly. I later realised that these convoys were quietly dropping off small groups of soldiers who hid in doorways to enforce the curfew.

This came home to me, quite forcibly one evening, when I was on the roof chanting '*Allah Akhbar!*' with the best of them and enjoying the view when there was a sudden, deafening volley of gunshots (I believe from my front doorstep) and a family leaning over the parapet on the roof opposite me, only fifty yards away, were shot and dropped several stories to the ground. I saw the whole thing; nobody came to help them and the bodies remained there until morning. We were later informed that the army considered that being in the open air was in breach of curfew… it could have been me.

By now the expats had formed a sort of telephone circle, and we kept in touch with each other outside office hours. Life in the office had become more difficult, with endless meetings of groups of Iranians in the office foyer, and some quietly disappearing abroad 'on holiday'.

Around this time, a small management group was formed in the OSCO Tehran office, and we spent many hours working out highly detailed (and secret) evacuation plans; thoroughly depressing work. We were only concerned with the logistics of moving the Tehran OSCO expatriates, as all the big decisions were being taken at the Ahwaz head office.

Shortly after the Christmas 'holiday' described above came the order to leave. Instructions were relayed round the expatriate telephone circle, and it was considered essential to keep the move absolutely secret from all Iranians in the office, including managers. So one day we worked in the office as normal, in the knowledge that, at dawn the next day, we were to sneak away without a word to anyone, and would not see the OSCO office again. That was a difficult day.

Car and apartment keys were left in designated places and we were allowed just one piece of baggage each; naturally everyone brought their biggest suitcase! Privately hired cars came to pick us up from our front doors and the idea was to move in convoy to the airport – quite a long drive. Though curfew hour had just passed, the streets were almost deserted as it was so early. But the trip wasn't easy; parts of our planned route were barricaded and some of the buildings were still burning – but we eventually made it to Mehrabad Airport.

This was a hive of army activity, but there were no scheduled flights anywhere, so we were alone in the large concourse, surrounded by stacks of metal ammunition and grenade boxes, and with soldiers busy doubling all over the place. They regarded us as a nuisance and we were told more that once to go away as there were no flights.

We had been told that an OSCO Fokker Friendship would come into Mehrabad and take us to Abadan. So we stood in a lonely circle for what seemed like hours. As the morning wore on, the fighting round the airport became quite intense; leaving its relative safety would not have been an option in any case. Unfortunately, the senior expatriate manager in charge, Dave, was completely drunk from the start and quite useless. There must have been more than fifty of us, including wives, and a couple of American teenage children with their father.

With the plane approaching, we were told how many it could carry and, of course, it could not take everyone in one trip. So began one of those hot air 'balloon' debates as to who got chucked over the side to keep it airborne and save all the others. I quickly retired from this – as a bachelor there was no way I was going to be on the first flight. So the decision was taken to take first all wives and their husbands, plus a few others who weren't too well. Two American children were kept back for the second flight with their father, and made a scene about it when they were told they were going to have to wait. To make matters worse, we were told that if we left our bags behind, several more could be taken on the plane. Remember there was no guarantee that it would come back... That was where Odette McMaster (Bill's wife) took control of the debate and persuaded everyone that, having got this far, we should all be allowed to take our bags. She was very courageous

143

throughout, and I have kept in touch with them at Christmas ever since.

The OSCO plane did get in, and I understood later that the captain had risked his licence by landing at an international airport without any clearance from the ground. There was no other air traffic and, I assume, nobody in the control tower; the whole place had become a huge army base. The pilot told those of us who remained that he would come back for us; we had no option but to take him at his word.

We waited for many hours without food or water, but late in the afternoon, lo and behold, that wonderful pilot did come back. We were so grateful as, from his perspective, he was landing in a 'war zone', which must have been daunting to say the least. So we made it to Abadan, and after a short wait, a Gulf Air 737 flew into Abadan and took us to Bahrain; there was spontaneous cheer as the aircraft lifted off from Iran. We then transferred to a Gulf Air TriStar for the onward flight to Athens. After having been without food and water, the Gulf Air flights were fantastic for their hospitality, first-class service and food all round – which I think the author of this book had organised – typical! Clearly, no budget worries!

And so on to Athens. Everything had been extremely well organised and I believe some 1,300 people (Iran's entire OSCO expatriate community) were accommodated in most of the five-star hotels in Athens. Unusually for Athens, the city was covered in snow in January, and very cold. But the amazing admin ensured that we all got a daily allowance and free taxis, plus briefings on what was happening back in Iran. The idea was to hold us there, ready to return as and when the situation allowed.

Despite the relative luxury, free meals etc., it became

quite boring and after about two weeks, one of my letters home said

> …with such a concentration of talented 'company men' here, some of them have been unable to resist organising things, forming committees, study groups, calling meetings etc. Such things blossom so quickly that, if we stay here much longer, we will have a large organisation, with everyone frantically busy, but with no end product!

Of course, after the Shah had left Iran and Ayatollah Khomeini's triumphant return to Iran from Paris, we were ultimately disbanded and those of us who were not direct hire were returned to our respective 'owners' (parent companies).

In May 1979, having been safely restored to home and work in the UK, I still felt guilty about the way we had left without saying a word to our Iranian friends. So I decided to go back to Tehran for a week at my own expense, just to say 'goodbye' properly. My employer, BP, was strongly against it and forbade me to go, saying that there was no insurance cover, or something. But I took some leave and got a BOAC flight to Tehran. When it arrived I was the only passenger to get off the plane there, and I have to admit that I was nervous. It was around this time that a TWA captain famously announced as he approached Mehrabad, 'Ladies and gentlemen, we are now about to land at Tehran Airport. Please put your watches back 600 years!'

I got into one of the usual orange-coloured Peykan taxis and asked to go to 'Avenue Shah'. The driver corrected me, saying that all the streets had new names, but he took me to the old OSCO office. I somewhat boldly walked inside to the reception desk, to be greeted with amazement by the security guards, '*Meestair Geelbairt!*' Also at the desk was a gowned mullah, who I gathered later was now running the show (!) and he apparently rushed back up to his office, pressed all his buttons and asked, 'Are they coming back?'

Anyway, I only wanted to go to the Contracts Department and also Personnel to get the keys to my flat. My own department could not believe it when I just walked in! So I promptly suggested a party at my place, a couple of days later. However, Carmen Lucassian, Hassan Mohebbi's secretary, wisely said that I could no longer just walk around the streets in safety, and insisted on driving me everywhere. She was right – nearly everyone, including women in chadors, were carrying modern guns, mostly looted from the army's armories, which had all been emptied by the mobs. At night there was quite a lot of shooting, and I imagine that old scores were being settled.

However, we did have a party, of sorts, in my fairly bare flat, with alcohol supplied by Hassan and Carmen. They presented me with a big filigree silver candelabra with everyone's initials engraved on the base. Thereafter, I returned to the UK, having said my farewell to Iran, and I still treasure that farewell gift.

Mike Hogg

Mike was a really old hand (though not in terms of years) when I joined OSCO early in 1975; a qualified quantity surveyor, the Newcastle-born Geordie left for Iran, on loan from his firm there, to a firm of architects, who in turn lent him on to IOEPC (now OSCO) for just a one-year contract. That was in February 1963, and he had been there ever since; he was originally based at Masjid-I-Sulaiman (MIS) – 'temple of Solomon' – where BP had first discovered oil in 1908.

By the time I arrived, Ahwaz had become the headquarters of the then named OSCO, and Mike and his wife, Diana, had been moved down from MIS to Ahwaz. Mike reported to Hooshang Ramhormozi, and so was part of my team. I have to say that his experience and dedication were quite outstanding and he was a pleasure to work with. Socially he was very active with the rugby club, the 'Hash House Harriers', the golf and squash club, amateur dramatics etc. – you name it, the Hoggs were always involved!

I also want to thank and pay tribute to him for all his help at the time of the evacuation; Mike was a cool-headed person to have in a crisis, and the work he did out at the airport in Ahwaz to get passengers loaded and flights away was outstanding. He says he does not remember much about it, but I don't believe him!

Here is what he has to say about our latter days in Iran:

During all the time I was living and working in Iran I felt it was a good place to be. While I was aware that it was a dictatorship, it appeared to be reasonably benign; women were liberated to the extent that they could wear what they pleased. I felt easy and safe travelling around the country, when visiting the capital Tehran and the ancient cities of Shiraz and Esfahan. There were even two breweries in the country making Shams and Mejidieh beer; it was certainly no closed Islamic society.

There was, of course, Savak lurking in the background; this was the Shah's domestic and intelligence security service. They had a reputation for the torture and execution of opponents of the Shah, although I was not aware of the extent of this.

In January 1978, for reasons that have always been unclear to me, there were demonstrations in Tehran calling for the overthrow of the Shah and his replacement with Ayatollah Khomeini, who had been exiled by the Shah in 1964. As the year progressed, the political situation gradually deteriorated and the demonstrations spread to other parts of the country. In August 1978 there was a fire in the Cinema Rex in Abadan in which 400 people were killed. Exactly who started the fire is not known, but it is thought that it may have been the religious authorities, in order to create a problem for the government.

Between August and December 1978 strikes and demonstrations paralysed the country. Eventually the Iranian oil workers who were working for OSCO went on strike. I remember going into the office each morning and the strikers were sitting on the floor of the main corridor shouting, 'Death to Americans!' I made it clear that I was British, not American!

The expatriate oil workers in Ahwaz all lived in privately owned housing in three locations – Melli Rah (affectionately known as 'Smelly Rah'), Kien Pars and

Kourosh. We were located in Melli Rah, and when the curfew was imposed by the authorities we were supposed to be confined to our houses. However, where we were, with mostly no guards, we were able to continue socialising.

Like most other people before the end of 1978, I assumed that everything would calm down and life return to normal; I expected that the Shah would reimpose his authority and all would continue as before.

The children of American oil workers remained in Iran for their secondary school education (at the American School in Tehran), while those of the other expats were sent off to boarding school. OSCO paid for two trips a year out to Iran for the children to come out and visit their parents. In spite of the political situation, Christmas/New Year 1978–9 was treated no differently from the norm, and to me this was indicative that the management assumed that the disturbances would cease and that the situation would, indeed, return to normal. Our children came out to join us, as usual, in mid-December to be with us over the holiday period. This meant that most expatriate children, both American and non-American, were in Ahwaz at that time.

Then, on Saturday, 23 December 1978, the American General Manager of Operations, Paul Grimm, was assassinated while driving himself to work after the Iranian weekend. He had been standing in for the OSCO Chairman, George Link (also an American), who had been pulled out by his company, Exxon, following an earlier attempt to blow up his car. This suddenly served to put a somewhat more serious aspect on matters.

A few days later, I heard that the order had been given to evacuate all expatriates and their families; I was not sure who was planning the whole operation, but I was asked to help with the evacuation and given a list of names of the oil workers, their wives and children, to be ticked off one by one as they left Ahwaz Airport. It was a case of women and children first – rather like a shipwreck.

OSCO operated its own fleet of aircraft, two F27 Fokker Friendships, two Twin Otters and a fleet of helicopters. The F27s took about thirty passengers and the Twin Otters about ten (at a push). These planes were used to evacuate the employees and their families from Ahwaz and the satellite settlements in Aga Jari, Gachsaran, Haft Kel, MIS and Naft Safid.

Being part of the evacuation organisation, I was on the last plane out on 7 January 1979. We flew first on OSCO's aircraft from Ahwaz to Abadan to collect the last of the evacuees from the other areas and from Abadan itself. I remember when we came to board the Gulf Air 737 at Abadan that we had to wait while someone negotiated with the pilot to bring his dog with him in the hold in place of his 'one suitcase' allowance. I think that he was successful, but whether or not the dog lived to tell the tale of the cargo hold, I know not.

The one person left was Jerry Gilbert, an OSCO reservoir engineer who had been taken to hospital in Abadan with hepatitis, and I did manage a quick visit to see him. He was a good friend of mine and tells his own story of how he got out in the next chapter.

Arriving in Bahrain we were put up overnight, and then Gulf Air flew us on to Athens, where all the other evacuees had been accommodated in various hotels. We made ourselves at home in Athens and used the same organisa-tional structure that had been in operation in Ahwaz for the evacuation to arrange various recreational and other activities. The non-American children returned to their respective schools as the spring term started. It was anticipated by the expats that, even if the Shah did leave and Khomeini came to power and settled in, all of us would return; how else could they run the oil industry?

The Shah fled Iran on 16 January 1979, with Khomeini arriving in Tehran in triumph a fortnight later on 1 February. He was declared the supreme spiritual leader. He introduced Sharia law, strictly enforced dress codes for men and women, and severely curtailed women's rights, freedom of speech and a free press.

It rapidly became apparent that any return to Iran was going to take longer than expected, so on 28 January all OSCO expatriate employees and their families in Athens were sent back to their 'point of origin', which, in my case, was Newcastle, from where I had left first in 1963 – sixteen years ago!

Although, one by one, direct hire employees were being laid off, I was asked to go into IROS in London and help out, along with Phil Watson and Bill Williams, to 'tidy up' and close out the contracts which OSCO had had with UK and other international contractors; each weekend I returned to Newcastle.

We were told that those of us being laid off would get their furniture and effects back, and that they had been packed up and shipped to a warehouse in Tehran. We then learnt that the warehouse had been set on fire and all the contents completely destroyed; it was a question then of getting people's inventories as best they could.

The expats who belonged to OSCO member companies, such as BP, were simply absorbed back into their own organisations. Direct hire personnel like me had to find themselves a new job, but we were given a terminal bonus of one month's salary for every year worked to cushion the blow and tide us over until we got new jobs.

The call for us to go back to Iran never came.

Jerry Gilbert – the Last Man Out

Jerry Gilbert was a BP secondee and worked as a planning manager, along with Bill Lloyd, in Ezzat Mazloomian's Planning Department. He was therefore a key figure in the logistics of analysing how many people were going to have to be evacuated, where they were all located, and how OSCO were going to assemble them all and move them down from Ahwaz to Abadan. Here is his remarkable story.

In early December 1978 it had been decided that contingency plans should be made to be ready, if and when the order to evacuate all OSCO personnel and their families was given. Bill Lloyd and I, in the Planning Department, started to set up an evacuation plan and helped to organise a street-by-street management–employee information system, so that all staff and families were kept aware of the political situation and a possible need for evacuation.

Prior to the full-scale evacuation, which was to follow after Christmas, we did try to get a few families out early while there was still the odd scheduled flight operating. I was at Ahwaz Airport, seeing a small group off on a flight, about 22 December, when my own two kids flew in from their Irish boarding school for their Christmas holidays!

The main evacuation started around 29 December, with families leaving Ahwaz, shuttling down to Abadan in the OSCO aircraft, and then on from there to Bahrain, flying on to Athens. About twelve of us were asked to stay on, so that OSCO did not void its agreement with NIOC by withdrawing all staff. The group included myself (BP), Mike Hogg (direct hire), Robin Scott and also Mike Hall (Shell, HR). I think that my main reason for staying was to protect a large shipment of beer that had recently been delivered to the rugby club, which I had founded a few years earlier! We did not feel in any danger at the time; popular opinion was still that the 'Revolution' would at last be suppressed by those forces still loyal to the Shah, and that all would return to normal within a month or two.

Around 4 or 5 January, with the evacuation well under way, having felt unwell for about ten days, but carrying on, I found a doctor who diagnosed that I had hepatitis. He arranged for an ambulance to take me to the hospital in Abadan, which was still functioning.

Around 7 January I had a brief visit from my good friends Mike Hogg and Robin Scott, who told me that they were on the way out, as all expatriate personnel were being pulled out; the situation in Ahwaz had deteriorated badly since I went into hospital. As their flight was about to leave, I started to get out of bed to join them, but was told that I had to stay in hospital and would be collected by a special flight when I had recovered; the Shell 'HR man' had told the others that it might be risky to have me travel with them, as I might infect them and all aboard the plane. I must have been very ill, as I accepted the order to stay without argument!

While I was in hospital, there was no way of contacting OSCO, BP or my family either by phone, telex or mail (which was not operating). I had no idea where my wife, Heather, and the kids were; similarly they had no idea exactly where I was and how I was faring.

Around 24 January, the hospital staff and Iranian and Pakistani nurses began to leave, as conditions in Abadan got worse, with sounds of gunfire at night etc. My nurses had looked after me well during the day, but when they went off duty they gathered outside my window, shouting, 'Death to the American!' – hard to explain that Ireland is not part of America! The hospital manager came and told me that I should leave, as he could no longer be responsible for me. He took my passport to the Iraqi Consulate in Abadan to obtain an entry visa – exiting Iran by land was now the only way out of the country. The airport runway had been blown up by the remnants of the Iranian army still loyal to the Shah to prevent Khomeini's entry, and the Gulf countries had closed their borders to people coming from Iran. The Iraqi Consul refused me a visa because, he said, Irish troops with the UN in Lebanon had killed Iraqis serving with Hezbollah there.

Around 28 January, conditions in the hospital worsened, with domestic staff leaving, and food and cleaning difficult. I was attacked in my bed by a patient, who came into my room and beat me with one of his crutches, while balancing on what was left of his legs and the other crutch. The hospital manager came in again and told me that I must leave, and he suggested that I should go and see the Iraqi Consul to plead, personally, for a visa. I was driven to the Consul; after some emotional discussion the Consul said that, if I apologised on behalf of my country, he would give me a visa. I was told to go on my knees and kiss his shoes; I did and my passport was stamped.

I was driven to the bridge at Khorramshahr (the border) and wheeled my meagre belongings across the river in a wheelbarrow. The Iraqi guards were surprised to see an expat, but were friendly enough – I spoke Arabic from a previous posting in Libya. They checked my bags and found many boxes of 35 mm slides, which I had brought down to

Abadan with me to sort out. They started looking at them, and soon there was a party, as they found photographs of my wife, Heather, and Diana Hogg and others in bikinis at the pump house pool and on some of our many camping trips. An hour or so passed and then they found a photo of me playing cricket at MIS; there were tanks in the background – the BMY factory at Naftak, where old Russian P38 tanks were being rebuilt for the Iranian army. The atmosphere changed in an instant; I was clearly a spy. An officer was sent for and I had a long and difficult session with him before I convinced everyone that I knew nothing about tanks, armies, or guns; then I was told that I could go.

I asked, on leaving, how I could get to Basra – a taxi, or a bus? The Iraqi border guards laughed. 'No one is crossing the border any more, so there is no transport; if you want to go to Basra, you should walk.'

So after three weeks in hospital, feeling pretty weak, I set off across the 25 km of desert to Basra. I got a few short lifts and eventually arrived at Basra Airport. Going to the ticket desk and asking for a flight to Baghdad and on to London, not an eyebrow was raised and I was asked how I would like to pay. I offered Iranian rials, which was all the cash I had, and was told that they were worthless. Then I remembered my American Express card, applied for a year ago and never used. Where could it be used in these days? I offered the card and it was accepted. I flew to Baghdad and then, after resting for three days, I flew on to London. I arrived at Heathrow to find that no one in BP had any idea what had happened to me, and didn't seem to have much interest either; I was not impressed!

Twenty years later, in May 1999, I returned to Ahwaz for two weeks as a member of BP's 'relationship-building' team, exchanging technical data with NIOC. I met many former (Iranian) reservoir engineering colleagues, and we had a warm reception from most NIOC management and staff – although one technical group refused to meet with us. I took the BP group down to the bazaar and we were warmly greeted and told we were welcome. I also went back to see my own and Mike Hogg's houses in Melli Rah. Climbing up the wall to look inside, neighbours appeared and asked what I was doing and who I was; after explanations I was invited in for a cup of *chai* (tea). The golf course had been built over with very basic housing and there were pools of stagnant water. Everywhere women seemed totally subjugated, and the shops were empty of anything except basic foodstuffs and clothing.

I flew out to Dubai in an Iran Air aircraft that was old and worn and I was very glad to land safely – but I am so pleased that I went back.

Paris and Total

I stayed on at the IROS offices for several weeks as a small team was being set up to deal with terminating the contracts of those international contractors who had being carrying out projects in Iran for OSCO and who had also had to pull out. This comprised Bill Williams, the OSCO General Manager of Finance (who had taken over from Sid Primrose), with Phil Watson, my BP Head of Contracts, Mike Hogg and several others.

I had started discussions with Total, my parent company, as to what was to become of me, and I flew over to Paris for interview at Total's headquarters, quite keen to leave Iran behind me. I had assumed that I would be posted to either their London office or up at the 'sharp end' in Aberdeen, from where Total's operations in the UK sector of the North Sea were run. However, as it turned out, they created a new post for me at the headquarters of Total Exploration and Development (TEPDD) based in the southern suburb of Pont de Sèvres, in Paris.

So after having a break and taking the children off to Davos for a skiing holiday, Ginny and I once again closed up our Teddington house and took Ginny's car on the cross-Channel ferry to start our new life in France. My appointment was *Directeur Commerciale*, and it appears I was the first non-French, non-*Ecole Polytechnique* graduate member of staff, and the only one on the TEPDD Board who did not have membership of the *Légion d'honneur* – a decoration I felt that I thoroughly deserved after helping to get all the expats out of Iran!

It rapidly became apparent that the logic behind my appointment was that it was thought that I could be a useful 'link' between TEPDD and the UK Department of Trade and Industry (DTI) and also the Offshore Supplies Office (OSO). Total had big ambitions of acquiring and developing more acreage in the UK sector of the North Sea, and they thought that it would look good to have a Scot on the Board who could help to deal with Total's relations with these powerful bodies; being (by now) bilingual was also a help.

It was a strange transition from OSCO as, although I had that grand-sounding title, I had no staff, except the use of a secretary, and my job description was very vague. I was only sent papers, memos and correspondence that my boss, Jacques, thought that I ought to see, or might be able to help with. Total were developing the large Alwyn Field and associated pipelines and terminals; the OSO was looking for all materials to be sourced in the UK, and for UK contractors to be awarded the construction projects – while Total strove for the very opposite! They wanted the steel purchased from Vallourec (the French steel mill), and French engineering companies involved in the design and construction phases. I had to become a bit of a diplomat in persuading the DTI and the OSO that the Alwyn and other projects were more likely to be brought in on time, and start yielding tax revenues to the UK Treasury earlier, if the French were allowed to 'do it their way'!

After a few weeks in a rather poorly furnished Total flat, we found a newly completed duplex apartment at Billancourt, just one metro stop north of Pont de Sèvres, and it was fun moving into that and getting it all furnished and sorted out. We had heard, by this time, that we would never see our furniture from Ahwaz, so we used our settlement payment from OSCO to furnish the Paris apartment. The duplex had quite a large roof garden area, already full of pretty poor soil and heavily overgrown. So we set to and picked out all the stones, rotavated it and sowed a lawn, putting roses and shrubs around the borders – all very odd, five stories up!

As well as dealing with the UK Sector of the North Sea, I was asked to help out occasionally in Abu Dhabi, where TEPDD were developing the Upper Zakum offshore field, so I made several trips there. Total considered that my previous experience in the Middle East would be helpful in negotiating some of the contracts there; it was pretty sporadic activity.

Being located in Paris, we obviously had a lot of visitors, and we developed a sort of 'tour' for them, usually ending up on a Saturday at Chartres, where there was an excellent local market and our guests could visit the absolutely stunning cathedral. Then we rounded it off with an excellent lunch at one of the really good restaurants there; not good for the figure, but I kept myself fit by still playing squash and jogging in the Bois de Boulogne.

On 4 November 1979 we heard of the 'sit-in' by Iranian extremists at the American Embassy, which quickly became a full-blown hostage crisis; we felt so sorry for all the American Embassy staff, as we had some inkling of what they would be experiencing. Having just begun to forget what we had been through, it all came flooding back, and President Carter looked pretty helpless as Khomeini refused to order the release of the Americans. Little did I know that this event was to come back to haunt me later on.

While I was enjoying being at TEPDD, I was bored; there really wasn't enough to do, after the life I had been used to. My boss, Jacques, sensed this and told me not to worry; they were very pleased that I was there when needed, but I should only come into the office 'as and when', for Board Meetings, and to look in on Thursdays to see if there was anything I needed to attend to. So the rest of 1979 and early 1980 passed with my walking to the office for a while, walking back to the apartment to have a relaxing lunch with Ginny, and only going back in the afternoon if I needed to. There are twenty-two public holidays in France, and many were on a Thursday, so you always took Friday off – *le pont* (bridge), as it was known. In addition I was entitled to six weeks' leave – so no problem going back to Davos for skiing at Easter!

We then heard, in April 1980, of the attempted military operation ordered by President Carter to rescue the American Embassy hostages still held in Tehran and how terribly badly it had gone wrong. Two helicopters didn't make it and a third collided with a C130, bursting into flames, with the loss of several American servicemen. Iran was still never out of our minds, and we thought of these poor hostages now dispersed into many locations in case there should be another 'rescue' attempt.

I had always kept in touch with my former OSCO boss, Malcolm Ford. When his tour at OSCO had come to an end in early 1978, he had become Managing Director of Shell Expro, responsible for Shell's operations in the North Sea. He was then moved over at the beginning of 1980 to become MD of the British National Oil Corporation (BNOC), taking over the running of that national organisation from Lord Kearton; BNOC was reputed to be in 'a bit of a muddle'.

I had a conversation with Malcolm sometime in May 1980 and mentioned to him that I was fine, but bored. As our discussion went on he said something like, 'James, you remember we thought we were badly organised in Iran – well, you should see this place! Would you be interested in coming to help me sort it out?'

So I took some of my available leave and flew over to Glasgow, for my 'second' interview with him at BNOC's Head Office in St Vincent Street. The rest, as they say, is history.

The British National Oil Corporation (BNOC)

There was the ideal job waiting for me at BNOC – to take over the running of Contracts, Procurement and Finance (except for Treasury). The fact that BNOC had its headquarters in Glasgow had been a political decision when this national company had been formed. It had to be a Scottish company, so had to have its headquarters in Scotland; Glasgow had pitched hard for it to be based there – and won. It was a most unfortunate decision, logistically; the sharp end of the business was up in Aberdeen, and all the other major oil companies had their UK head offices in London; so I ended up with a third of my department in Glasgow, a third in Aberdeen and the remaining third in London – crazy!

I was back in my element, with a substantial number of staff spread out over the three offices; contracts for drilling rigs, onshore and offshore installation projects (the Beatrice Field being but one), and a contract to build the Ocean Alliance Semi-submersible deep water drilling rig, which can operate in 4,000 feet of water and drill to a 25,000 foot depth. Also in procurement, we were back buying line pipe, but this time having our arm twisted by the OSO to give the contract to British Steel.

Sir Ian Macgregor was the chairman at the time, and I remember meeting him when he said they would 'try' to meet our very stringent specification; it took them several hundred lengths of condemned pipe before they got it right. I also had the Finance Department to look after and another

Watson; this time 'Ron' was my Finance Manager and a tower of strength, highly capable and a pleasure to work with; I was very grateful for his support, as having Finance as well under my wing was something new.

However, Iran then came back into our lives with the establishment of the Iran Arbitration Tribunal in The Hague, which, as I understand it, was part of the 'deal' relating to the ultimate release of the American Embassy hostages in Tehran. As the months passed, they had become an embarrassment to Khomeini; he could not just back down and send them home, but looking after them in various locations and keeping them was increasingly damaging to Iran's image, not only in the Western world, but among Arab nations in the Middle East; Iranian crude oil output, such as it was, had been embargoed in many countries.

I had been told that all the files in my office in Ahwaz had been moved up to the Iranian Revolutionary Council in Tehran shortly after I had left, and it was these that came back to haunt me as part of the Hague arbitration proceedings. On 21 January 1981, the fifty-two American hostages held at the time of the siege of the American Embassy in Tehran had been released, after 444 days in captivity. Iran had finally agreed to free the hostages, after the US said it would release assets frozen in American banks, including also an agreement with the UK to release Iranian investments/assets there. As I recall, another stipulation was the establishment of a tribunal in The Hague under the international arbitration procedures, to deal with outstanding claims that Iran viewed it had. It seemed to be all about 'reparation' for the alleged 'excesses' of the oil majors, while in Iran, for awarding overly lucrative contracts to American, British and other international construction companies, to the detriment of local Iranian (alleged) capability.

So I suddenly had copies of many of the major contracts that I had signed under a Power of Attorney with Brown & Root, Fluor, Parsons, Kellog, Foster Wheeler etc. sent to me by their lawyers. I was asked/required to draft, complete and sign sworn affidavits with a justification explaining not only why these contracts had been awarded, but defending the commercial terms agreed as not being excessively generous. It was very strange, years later, to have your own signature put in front of you at the end of a document and justify, in detail, the award of the contract in the first place and the contract terms. I do not think that my affidavits endeared me to the Iranians and their lawyers on the other side of the arbitration.

On moving back to the UK, as my base was to be in Glasgow with BNOC, it seemed logical to move to Scotland. We had sold our house in Teddington, and I had asked my brother to look out for somewhere near him and not far from my sister. He sent me a newspaper cutting of a house for sale while we were still in France; Ginny and I flew over and immediately fell in love with it. The house had four bedrooms, a large garden, and a staff flat and nursery wing, which was to be ideal for Ginny's father to come and live in, as he was getting pretty elderly.

After we had moved in, and I had given all the evidence that I could to the Iran arbitration tribunal in The Hague, we thought that Iran was, finally, behind us. We came in one evening after being out to dinner with friends; I went to look at the answerphone and the red light was flashing with a message to read. I turned on the 'playback' and the voice said:

'This is the Iranian Revolutionary Council in Tehran, with a message for Mr James Lawson. We want to advise you that we know exactly where you are.'

Acknowledgements

I would like to thank the following for their help, guidance and assistance in the writing of this book: Vanessa French, of British Petroleum (BP) Pensions, whom I first contacted (as a BP pensioner), for giving me useful contacts and support; Peter Housego, Global Archive Manager of BP Archives, University of Warwick, whose research in retrieving the exchange of telexes at the time relating to the evacuation was invaluable; Anthony (Tony) Gilbert, Mike Hogg and Jerry Gilbert, for their contributions to this book; all the management and staff of Athena Press for their help and guidance in editing the book and bringing it to fruition; and finally my darling wife, Ginny, without whose persistence and help this short book would never have seen the light of day.

Appendix 1

Inward Message　　　　| ACTION: 　　　　　　　| CC: 　　　　　／ |

WXPC1360
FROM OILSERVCO AHWAZ GM(O)
TO IROP LONDON (GLOSS)

CONFIDENTIAL

NO.AZ43144　　　　30,9,57(21,12,78)　　　　17:25

NIOC RUSH OIL CABLE 20/12/78 FROM AZIMI NIOC MKTG.

EYES ALONE CABLE FACILITIES NOT AVAILABLE IOP WAS SENT CABLE FROM
AZIMI STATING NORMAL KHARG LOADING PROCEDURES TO DETERMINE SEQUENCE
IN QUEUE SHOULD BE ALTERED TO ALLOW LISTED VESSELS LOADING
NIOC PARCELS TO BE LOADED BY 31 DEC. 1978. URGENTLY REQUIRE
MEMBERS RESPONSE TO THIS CABLE. INFORMED KHARG NOT TO CHANGE
SEQUENCE UNTIL ADVISED BY MEMBERS THAT AGREEMENT REACHED WITH NIOC.
BASED ON CURRENT ESTIMATES OF RECEIPTS AT KHARG AND PRESENT
SEQUENCE WORLD CONQUERER, NORDIC SKY (WHICH IS NOT EVEN AT
ANCHORAGE), WOLFEN, SEA SONG, JAPAN ADONIS (IL ONLY), AJDABYA,
HEINSDORF (NO CARGO NOMINATED AS YET) AND LANINA COUWD NOT BE
LOADED AS REQUESTED UNLESS SEQUENCE ALTERED WITH MEMBERS
APPROVAL. CAN MEMBERS DISCUSS WITH NIOC AND AGREED SEQUENCE BE
FURNISHED KHARG SOONEST.
NEW SUBJECT: GASHSARAN .26 IN. MOL FROM PU-1 AND PU-2 TO GURREH
WAS BLOWN UP BY SABATEURS AT 2130 HRS. 20/12/78. PRODUCTION OF
359 MBPD IH CURTAILED UNTIL LINE REPAIRED. ESTIMATE 24 HRS.
REQUIRED TO REPAIR. NO ARRESTS MADE NOR ANY DETAILED INFORMATION
AVAILABLE AS YET. POINT OF BLAST WAS CONFLUENCE OF THREE LINES
NEAR BRIDGE WHICH COULD HAVE INTERRUPTED ENTIRE GASHSARAN
PRODUCTION IF ALL LINES PARTED AS WAS PROBABLY THE PLAN.
GS PRODUCTION IS 545MBPD. DOWN FROM 911 MBPD 20/12/78.
. . . .
SMF
NNNN

1430/21.12.78

MR GLOSS　2
MR LEE　　5
NORMAL CIRCULATION
MR PORTER 2
MR BAYMAN 2

Appendix 2

| ACTION: | CC: / |

TO IROP LONDON FOR GLOSS FROM LINK (PEG)

E Y E S   A L O N E

A743150   22.12.78

ON 20.12.78 DELEGATION OF ABOUT TEN IRANIAN STAFF DELIVERED
MASS RESIGNATION LETTER TO RAOOFI DATED 19.12.78.   THE MASS
RESIGNATION LETTER IN THE FORM OF A PETITION CONTAINED A
PREFACE CITING REASONS FOR THE ACTION AND ATTACHED SHEETS OF
SIGNATURES AND REGISTRATION NUMBERS REPORTED TO ME AT 1800
HRS. 21.12.78 BY RAOOFI AS TOTALING 540 INDIVIDUALS FROM
BROAD COVERAGE OF DEPARTMENTS OF WHICH 430 WERE STAFF AND
110 WERE DRE'S. DRILING DIVISION HAD EARLIER REPORTED
INFORMATION THAT 94 OF THEIR STAFF AND DRE'S HAD SIGNED A
MASS RESIGNATION WHICH PRESUMABLY IS A PART OF THOSE HANDED
RAOOFI. DRILLING STAFF INVOLVED WERE PRINCIPALLY RIG SUPT.
TRAINEES AND MUD MEN TRAINEES. RAOOFI TOLD ME THAT NAGHSHINEH,
SERAJI AND HE HAD MADE DECISION TO HAVE SERAJI COMPOSE LETTER
TO EACH INDIVIDUAL ON LIST ADVISING THEM THAT THEY WERE STILL
CONSIDERED OSCO EMPLOYEES SUBJECT TO RULES AND REGULATIONS
GOVERNING THEIR EMPLOYMENT UNTIL SUCH TIME AS THEY SUBMITTED
AN INDIVIDUAL LETTER OF RESIGNATION. THIS IS CONTRARY TO
RECOMMENDATION MADE EARLIER BY EVANS AND ME WHEN RUMOR OF
SUCH ACTION WAS FIRST UNCOVERED. OUR RECOMMENDATION WAS TO
ACCEPT RESIGNATIONS THEREBY ESTABLISHING CLEAN BREAK WITH
RESPECT TO SALARY AND OTHER BENEFITS, WHICH WOULD HAVE PLACED
SOME ECONOMIC STRAIN ON THOSE PEOPLE. WE WOULD THEN CONTACT

                              CONT'D ....

THOSE INDIVIDUALS WHOM WE ACTUALLY WISHED TO RETAIN AND
ADVISE THEM WE WOULD ACCEPT A LETTER FROM THEM RECINDING
THEIR RESIGNATION.

TODAY INFORMED THAT ABOUT 150 OF THE 540 TOTAL WERE
TECHNICIANS WITH LESS THAN SIX MONTHS SERVICE AND THAT
RAOOFI HAS AGREED TO DISCHARGE 20 TO 30 PER CENT OF
THESE, SAY 30 TO 40 PEOPLE, SOME FROM EACH OF THE DIVISIONS,
TO IMPRESS OTHERS THAT A RESIGNATION IS A SERIOUS MATTER.

NEW SUBJECT:

AGHA JARI STILL IS AREA OF MOST CONCERTED STRIKE ACTION.
TODAY'S PRODUCTION, 22.12.78, IS FROM THREE PU'S BUT TOTALS
ONLY 106 MBPD. RAOOFI AND NAGHSHINEH VISITED AJ 20.12.78
AND REPORTEDLY AGREED TO DISCHARGE OF 12 PEOPLE IDENTIFIED
AS HARD CORE STRIKERS. NONE OF THESE PEOPLE HAVE BEEN FOUND
TO ADVISE THEM OF THEIR DISCHARGE.

CONT'D.....

PAGE THREE/PC1351

26 IN. MOL BREAK AT GACHSARAN STILL NOT REPAIRED. ANTICIPATE
ANOTHER 36 HRS. BEFORE WORK CAN BE COMPLETED. DELAY CAUSED
BY CONTINUING DRAINAGE FROM BROKEN LINE ESTIMATED TO TOTAL
100 MB.

MEETING WITH GOVERNOR GENERAL AND MILITARY HAS RESULTED IN
ASSIGNMENT OF 24 HRS. GUARDS AT VULNERABLE RIVER CROSSINGS
AND MOL PETROLS. DETAILS OF EVENT WHICH PARTED 26 INCH
MOL INDICATE DYNAMITE CHARGES WERE SET UNDER EACH OF THREE
LINES, ONE 24 INCH AND TWO 26 INCH, WHERE THEY PASS UNDER
BRIDGE NEAR JUNCTION GACHSARN/GURREH ROAD AND PAZANAN ROAD.
ALL CHARGES EXPLODED. THE 24 INCH LINE HAS DENT 8 INCH DEEP
BY 18 INCH LONG. THE OTHER 26 INCH LINE ALSO HAS LARGE
DENT. BOTH WILL HAVE TO BE REPAIRED BUT AT MORE APPROPRIATE
TIME.

NEW SUBJECT:
HAVE TOLD KHARG NOT TO CHANGE LOADING SEQUENCE OTHER THAN
ADVISED PER ESSO WILHELMSHAVEN AND ARISTOTLE ONASIS UNTIL
MEMBERS RESPOND.

                         MR GLOSS   2
                         NORMAL CIRCULATION
                         MR PORTER   2
                         MR BAYMAN   2

. . .
AD.

0900/22/12.

Appendix 3

ACTION: CC: /

PC 1352

FROM OILSERVCO AHWAZ
TO IROP LONDON FOR 6LONG FROM NAGSHINEH

A7 43169 / 23/12/78

IT IS WITH DEEP SORROW THAT WE HAVE TO INFORM YOU THAT THIS
MORNING AT 0700 HRS PAUL GRIMM WAS AMBUSHED AT THE CORNER OF
EGHBAL STREET AND MIS HIGHWAY, ON THE WAY TO OFFICE AND
FATALLY SHOT. I HAVE ASKED TOM EVANS TO LOOK AFTER MRS. GRIMM.
THE BODY IS BEING PREPARED FOR TRANSFER TO THE U.S.
MR AND MRS BUSH WILL ACCOMPANY MRS GRIMM AND POSSIBLY THE BODY.
WILL PROVIDE MORE DETAILS AS SOON AS THEY BECOME AVAILABLE.

AT ABOUT THE SAME TIME MR. BOROOJERDI ZONE SUPERINTENDENT OF
AHWAZ EAST PRODUCTION WAS ALSO FATALLY SHOT IN HIS CAR IN FRONT
OF HIS HOUSE IN KIAN PARS AREA.

NIOC AND MEMREP OFFICE WERE NOTIFIED IMMEDIATELY.

PLEASE NOTIFY GEORGE LINK OF THESE INCIDENTS.

...
GJP

0820/23.12.

RELAYED TO
MEMREP TEHERAN
BY LR 840.

Appendix 4

Inward Message

ACTION: CC: /

PC 1353

FROM OILSERVCO AHWAZ

TO IROP LONDON FOR GLOSS FROM EVANS

I M M E D I A T E

AZ 43207   23/12/78

FURTHER OUR PC 1352 FLIGHT DETAILS OF MR AND MRS BUSH AND MRS
GRIMM AND MR GRIMM'S BODY AS FOLLOWS. THEY WILL ALL DEPART
FROM ABADAN TOMORROW 24/12 ON IR 755 AT 1015 HRS AND CONNECT
TW 701 FROM LONDON TO JFK AIRPORT IN NEW YORK. AS DISCUSSED
WITH TOM SUMMERS PLEASE HAVE APC IN NEW YORK MEET THEIR FLIGHT,
MAKE ARRANGEMENTS FOR POSSIBLE OVERNIGHT STAY IN NEW YORK AND
STORAGE OF BODY, AND ASSIST IN OBTAINING TICKETS TO EITHER
CONNECTICUT OR DENVER, COLORADO DEPENDING ON WHAT GRIMM'S
NEXT OF KIN WILL DECIDE PERTAINING TO PLACE OF BURIAL.

...
·GJP

1145 | 23·12

MR. GLOSS 2.
NORMAL CIRC
MR. PORTER 2
MR. BAYMAN 2

Outward Message

ACTION: | CC: /

612034 OSCO IR

884784 IRANOL G

N.B. THIS MESSAGE ALSO PASSED ON THE DIRECT LINE TO AHWAZ

TELEX OPERATOR PLEASE PASS THIS MESSAGE TO MR EVANS IMMEDIATELY
===

FROM IROP LONDON   1520/24/12/78

TO   OILSERVCO AHWAZ
      TO MR EVANS FROM MR GLOSS

LDN 20498   24.12.78

WOULD YOU PLEASE TELEPHONE ME IMMEDIATELY.
THANKYOU.

...
BS

DIST:- MR GLOSS 2

612034 OSCO IR

884784 IRANOL G

Appendix 5

Inward Message

SC?0730   PC 1354   ACTION: CC:

FROM OILSERVCO AHWAZ GLM/3-MGL
URGENT TO IROS LONDON FOR RELAY TO EXXON CORP.

NEW YORK ATT: ESSO MIDDLE EAST
MESSRS: W.D.KRUGER
J.BURRIS
COPY IRAP LONDON ATT: CRUTCHFIELD EXXON LDN

NO.A74:3231   3.10.57(24.12.78)   08:40

RECENT EVENTS IN AHWAZ RESULTS IN DETERIORATION OF
MORALE OF SOME PERSONNEL(.) CURRENT SITUATION APPEARS
NOT ACCEPTABLE TO SOME EXXON PERSONNEL(.)
URGENT THAT YOU ADVISE SOONEST(.)
REGARDS
E.H. HANKS- GLM/3
TELEPHONE:
HOME - 2370
OFFICE-2569
...
HH

NN

0600/24/12/78

RELAYED TO
EXXON CORP
NYK & (86s)
EXXON LONTON
@. 0740/24.12.78

MR GROSS   2
+ NORMAL.
MR PORTER   2
MR BRYMAN   2

Appendix 6

Inward Message | ACTION: | CC: /

PC1357   SC20764
FROM OILSERVCO AHWAZ   GMT -GMA-MPN-PNA
IMMEDATELY TO IROP LONDON FOR ATTENTION MR. GLOSS
IMMEDATELY COPY IROS LONDON

NO. A743283   3.10.57(24.12.78)   17.10

FAMILY REPATRIATION

AYE: WE HAVE FORTY-ONE(41) FAMILY MEMBERS PLUS THREE(3)
     EMPLOYEES (PROCEEDING ON EARLY LEAVE) TRAVELLING ON
     THE SPECIAL AIR TRANSPORT YOU ARRANGED(.)
     ETD FROM ABADAN WILL BE AROUND 2030 HOURS LOCAL TIME
     (1700 GMT)(.) AS ALL FLIGHT ARRANGEMENTS MADE YOUR
     SIDE . WE CANNOT GIVE IDEA OF ETA LONDON(.) DETAILS
     PER FINAL DESTINATIONS WILL BE ADVISED BY TELEX LATER
     TO DAY (.)

BEE: ORIGINAL OF MORTUARY CERTIFICATE (COPY ALREADY TELEXED
     YOURS) AS REQUIRED FOR BODY OF MR. GRIMM IS BEING
     CARRIED SAFEHAND OF MR. GASH(.)

... 1442|24.12

MS

NNNN

MR GLOSS 2
NORMAL CIRC
MR BAYMAN 2
MR PORTER 2

Inward Message

ACTION: CC:

358   SC20765
FROM OILSERVCO AHWAZ   GMT-GMA-MPN-PNA-PL/2
IMMIDIATE TO IROP LONDON   ATTN MR GLOSS
IMMIDIATE TO IROS LONDON

NO. AZ43286   3/10/57 (24/12/78)   1930

FAMILY REPATRIATION
FOLLOWING IS LIST OF EMPLOYEES AND/OR FAMILY MEMBERS
WITH DESTINATIONS TRAVELING ON SPECIAL GULFAIR FLIGHT

REG NO.	NAME	AGE	DESTINATION
T OSCO	DITLAND		HOUSTON
	MR L		
	MRS R		
	MR D		
	CYR		SAN FRANCISCO
	MRS S		
00619	RICHARDS		SEATTLE
	MRS P		
	DECKER		
	MR D	15	
	MR T	13	
00462	CORRIGAN		MONTROSE COLO
	MISS C		VIA DENVER
00616	BARKLEY		MIDLAND TEX
	MRS J		
	MR K	16	

CONT/...

```
05076      BRADY                    MIDLAND TEX
           MRS S
           MISS C    13
07108      PRAUGHT                   HALIFAX CAN
           MRS N
           MR T
           MISS L
           MISS C
00073      JARAMILLO                 PADUCAH KY
           MRS C
           MISS C    14
00232      SVENNINGSEN               EDMONTON CAN
           MRS A
           MISS L    9
           MR R      14
00384      FERGUSON                  CALGARY
           MRS E
             MISS M    17
             MISS D    15
00375      FORSTER                   MANCHESTER
           MR WT
           MRS E
           MISS   L   12
             MISS S    3
           MR H       9
           MR   S     6
                                KONT/...
```

PAGE THREE OF PC1358 SC20765

```
00522   BARRETT                    LONDON
        MR  R
        MRS
        THREE CHILDREN
00096   RENAUD                     LONDON
         MRS B
00221   GASH                       MANCHESTER
        MR  B
        MRS M
        MR  D      3
        MISS L     2
00431   NIETO                      BOGOTA  CO
        MRS G
        MR  P      6
        MUSS J     5
        MISS  O    2
...
         1645/24.12.
```

MR GROSS 2.
NORMAL CIRC
MR BAYMAN 2
MR PORTER 2:

Appendix 7

Inward Message

ACTION:	CC:	/

FROM OILSERVCO AHWAZ
TO IRANOP LONDON
COPY TO MENREP TEHRAN FOR GLOSS/ORANGE FROM EVANS

RE YOUR LDN 20657 28/12/78

IN VIEW OF IRAN AIR STRIKE AT PRESENT WE CANNOT ASSURE THAT ANY
GROUND SUPPORT FACILITIES WILL BE AVAILABLE INCLUDING FUEL AND
THAT INCLUDES ANY ASSISTANCE FROM OSCO ABADAN. AT THIS STAGE
AIRCRAFT SHOULD AS FAR AS POSSIBLE BE SELF SUPPORTING AND RECKON
ON REFUELLING ELSEWHERE.
THERE ARE NO INTERNATIONAL FLIGHTS COMING IN TO ABADAN AS ALL
GROUND HANDLING IS DONE BY IRAN AIR.

...

1300/28.12.78

MR GLOSS 2
NORMAL CIRC.
MR PORTER 2
MR BAYMAN 2

Relayed MENREP under
LL0862 1305/28.12

Outward Message

ACTION:	CC: /

FROM: IRANOP LONDON

TO OILSERVCO AHWAZ FOR EVANS FROM GLOSS

LDN 20736 29/12/78

    I HAD A LONG TELEPHONE CALL WITH MAJID DIBA THIS MORNING
AND ADVISED HIM OF THE ARRANGEMENTS THAT WE WERE MAKING.
HE INDICATED THAT HE WILL DO HIS BEST TO ASSIST IN
OBTAINING LANDING PERMITS AS SOON AS HE HAS THE NECESSARY
INFORMATION. I AM ATTEMPTING TO GET THIS TO HIM AS SOON
AS POSSIBLE.
    IN OUR DISCUSSION DIBA EXPRESSED AN INTEREST IN OSCO
TRANSPORTING THE FAMILIES OF NIOC EXPATRIATE EMPLOYEES
NOT ONLY TO ATHENS BUT ONWARD TO LONDON. I ADVISED HIM THAT
IF THIS WAS WHAT NIOC WANTED WE WOULD CERTAINLY DO IT.
...
PW

SENT AHWAZ AT ...1020/29

MR GLOSS 2 / NORMAL CIRC.
MR PORTER 2 / MR BAYMAN 2

Appendix 8

Inward Message | ACTION: | CC: |

O OPERATOR ARE YOU THERE PLEASE ?

28))

WILL YOU PLEASE INFORM MESSRS GLOSS/ PORTER THAT BOTH MR EVANS
AND MYSELF CAN BE CONTACTED BY PHONE THROUGH AZ   31383 WHICH

IS HOME OF MR LUCAS OR THROUGH FHONE OF MR CRITES NO 35407

PLEASE ASK MR GLOSS HOW LONG HE WOULD LIJ LIKE THIS LINE KEPT

OPEN TO DAY

1301/28.12

MR GLOSS 1
MR PORTER 2

Inward Message

ACTION: CC: /

STF TLX 103 292248 LNN083 292248 ..NO SOM
PARSONS PSD B

29 DECEMBER 1978   2:39 P   *Relayed*

IRANIAN OIL SERVICE

LONDON, ENGLAND   *unisse → LON*

FOR RELAY TO OILSERVCO AHWAZ, IRAN *Relayed*   LR 884

29626   *memcefunder*

RESPONDING TO OILSERVCO TELEX 884958/884784 IRANOL G. FROM EVANS/
LAWSON FOR RELAY TO PARSONS PASADENA, ATTENTION OF W. E.
LEONHARD AND BILL HANNA:

PLEASE BE ADVISED THAT FOLLOWING RECEIPT OF LATER INFORMATION,
PARSONS HAS ORDERED REPATRIATION ONLY FOR DEPENDANTS OF ITS
EXPATRIATE EMPLOYEES.

PARSONS' ASST. MANAGER OF SITE OPERATIONS WHO IS PRESENTLY IN
CHARGE AT THE SITE IS BEING ADVISED THAT IT IS PARSONS' DESIRE
WITH CONDITIONS PERMITTING TO RETAIN AT THE SITE SUCH STAFF AS
ARE NECESSARY FOR THE SUPPORT OF THE PROJECT, AND THAT FURTHER
DECISIONS RESPECTING ORDERS FOR REPATRIATION WILL BE MADE
BY HIM WITHIN THE CONTEXT OF PARSONS' WISHES AND AS CONDITIONS
DICTATE.

THE ASST. SITE MANAGER IS BEING INSTRUCTED TO MAINTAIN MAXIMUM
POSSIBLE COORDINATION WITH AVAILABLE OSCO PERSONNEL REGARDING
PARSONS' ACTIVITIES IN THESE RESPECTS. ALTHOUGH THE REFERENCED
TELEX ADVISED THAT THE CAMP CONTINUES TO BE UNDER MILITARY

GUARD. PARSONS IS INFORMED THAT MILITARY PROTECTION HAS BEEN
REMOVED FROM RESIDENTIAL AREAS AND FROM PARSONS' OFFICE.
THIS FACT TOGETHER WITH THE ACTUAL ASSAULTS UPON PARSONS'
PERSONNEL AND THE GENERAL STRIFE AND DISORDER WHICH REPORTEDLY
IS CONTINUING IN THE AHWAZ AREA IS CAUSING A SUBSTANTIAL NUMBER

OF EXPATRIATE PERSONNEL TO HAVE EXTREME CONCERN FOR THEIR
FETY. YOU WILL, ACCORDINGLY, APPRECIATE THAT ALTHOUGH PARSONS
MAY NOT ORDER OR AUTHORIZE ALL PERSONNEL TO LEAVE, IT IS NOT

WITHIN ITS RIGHT OR POWER TO COERCE INTO REMAINING THOSE
PERSONNEL WHO OUT OF CONCERN FOR THEIR SAFETY WISH TO DEPART
OF THEIR OWN VOLITION. IN THIS CONNECTION, WE HAVE BEEN INFORMED
THAT CERTAIN PERSONNEL HAVE ALREADY MADE THEIR OWN DECISION TO DEPART
PARSONS' ABILITY TO MAINTAIN STAFF WILL BE FURTHER IMPERILED AND

ULTIMATELY MADE IMPOSSIBLE UNLESS THE CURRENT FAILURE TO PROVIDE

THE ADVANCE FUNDS REQUESTED UNDER PARSONS' REQUESTS OF NOVEMBER 27

AND DECEMBER 19 IS QUICKLY REMEDIED. IN THAT CONNECTION,

WE ARE GRATIFIED TO HAVE BEEN ADVISED BY IROS PERSONNEL IN LONDON
TODAY THAT THEY WOULD EXERT EVERY EFFORT ON OUR BEHALF TO EXPEDITE
THESE ADVANCES AND FUTURE ADVANCE FUNDINGS OF IN-COUNTRY

COSTS, AND WE ANTICIPATE THEIR BEING ABLE TO DO SO.

IN CONCLUSION, WE INTEND TO DO ALL THAT IS REASONABLY POSSIBLE
TO CONTINUE THE SUPPORT OF THE PROJECT IN LIGHT OF THE
CIRCUMSTANCES.

T.W. COOPER, PROJECT SITE MANAGER
PARSONS OVERSEAS COMPANY

PARSONS PASADENA
TLX 675336

5545-1   01-9110

SENT ONE END KB

PARSONS PSD B

.....
ABOVE SENT VIA ITT 12/29/78 1748 EST FROM PARSONS PSD B

MR PORTER
MR GLOSS 2,   MA
MR BAYMA   2,

Appendix 9

Inward Message

ACTION: CC: /

205/05.58
664358 IRANOL G

WARWTP APLE GR
2020 30 DECEMBER
FOR PORTER FROM BAYMAN

THE FOLLOWING STAFF/FAMILIES ARRIVED SAFELY IN ATHENS AT 2145
HOURS GMT 50TH DECEMBER. IN LIAISON WITH APC PLEASE ADVISE NEXT
OF KIN/CONTACT ADDRESS. YOU WILL OF COURSE NEED TO MAKE THE
POINT THAT STAFF ARE REMAINING I N ATHENS 2/3 WEEKS OR OTHERWISE
RESATIVES WILL ASSUME THEY ARE TRAVELLING ON.

U1508	MR AND MRS HVR JONES + 1
U1504	MR TRENAMAN
00507	MR PARDO
00018	MR RIGG
00868	MR CRAIGN
00855	MR FLETCHER
00050	MR AND MRS PRESHO
00850	MR D JONES
00040	MR AND MRS GULLIVER +2
02554	MC UMR AND MRS DOWNER +2
.0144	MR AND MRS CHUN +2
07004	MR AND MRS CRITES +1
00222	MR AND MRS HUSKINS + 2
02454	MR AND MRS WEGMANN +2
00070	MR AND MRS PETURSSON + INFANT
00542	MR DAVISON
U1401	MR AND MRS PARKINSON
U1507	MR BROADLEY
(CONTINUED)....	

PAGE TWO....

01473	MR AND MRS SCOTT +2
00052	MRS LAWSON
02472	MR SELIS
00550	MRS WEDLAKE
02461	CS MRS HALE + 4
07110	MRS WILLIAMS + 4
00854	MR WARMACK
00044	MR AND MRS ARNESKANS + 5
00115	MR AND MRS PATRICK - MITCHINSON + 2
01555	MR AND MRS FRASER
01515	MR ENGLISH
00057	MR EVANS
01515	MR HARRIS
00257	MR BONSALL
00503	MR JOHNSON
00354	MR AND MRS ORWIN + 1
01505	MR AND MRS ALLINSON
00457	MR AND MRS WATKIN + 2
00750	MR AND MRS PHILLIPS
00110	MR AND MRS WAKE
	MRS DARBY + 5 WIFE OF REV DARBY
	MRS HALE + 5

+++

THANK YOU

0800/ 31/12/78

MR PORTER 2
MR GLOSS 2
10P NORMAL.
MR BAYMAN 2.

Appendix 10

Inward Message   ACTION: CC: /

FROM OILSERVCO AHWAZ
TO IROS LONDON FOR PORTER FROM EVANS.

URGENT URGENT URGENT

WE ARE HAVING SEVERE LOGISTICAL PROBLEMS WITH OUR TEHRAN
PEOPLE BEING REPATRIATED. WE HOPE TO MOVE ABOUT THIRTY TO
ABADAN/BAHRAIN TODAY AND THE REST TOMORROW. HOWEVER THIS IS VERY
LIKELY TO FALL APART AND THEREFORE YOU ARE MOST URGENTLY
REQUESTED TO TRY TO OBTAIN A LANDING PERMIT FOR ONE GULF AIR /51
FOR TOMORROW MONDAY FIRST JANUARY.
WE WILL WORK ON IT THIS END ALSO.

. . .

083/31
PHONED PORTER

MR PORTER 2
MR BAYMAN 2
MR LEE 5
MR GROSS 2
NORMAL CIR.

Appendix 11

Inward Message   ACTION: _____ CC: _____ / _____

OK THANKS   WELLL RCD
FROM LAWSON TO MR GLOSS
GLAD TO SAY THE TABLETS HAVE ALREADY ARRRIVED IN ABDAN AND
ARE UN HANDS OF   MR CAMERON HD AVIATION OSCO THEY ARE BEING
FLOWN UP TO ME   TOMORRROW . BANG GOES MY LAST EXCUSE FOR LEAVING

1450/31.

Appendix 12

FROM IROS LONDON PORTER

TO OILSERVCO AHWAZ CARLTON

EYES ALONE

==========

GP1   2/1/79·   *Staying on*

REFERENCE LIST YOU SENT YESTERDAY PLEASE CONFIRM WE HAV
CORRECTLY IDENTIFIED THE FOLLOWING

AHWAZ	REGISTERED NO	AFFILIATION
C.T. EVANS	05148	MOBIL
J.A.D. CRAWFORD AND WIFE	00958	MOBIL
J.H. LAWSON	08032	CFP
M.R. HOGG	00642	D/H B
C.M. JOLLY	00440	D/H B
J.F.K. WILLIAMS AND WIFE	05070	TEXACO
F.J. MEIER	05147	MOBIL
J.D. BENNAT	00455	D/H A
G. BIRTWHISTLE	00582	D/H C
H.V. EHRENREICH	00472	D/H D
J.G. BRADY	05076	TEXACO
W.H. CRITES	07084	GULF
D. HAW	01481	BP
R.G. SPEERS	01450	BP
(CONTINUED)		

PAGE TWO GP1

M.G. O'DONNEL	01511	BP
R. SCHENK	04152	SOCAL
C.E. GUIN	00780	D/H A
F. TARE	00794	D/H C
R GOODNIGHT	00726	D/H A
M. BAXTER	00820	D/H A
J. J. GILBERT	01421	BP
C.E. PHILLIPS	00750	D/H A
J PATTIS	00441	D/H A
T.H. DALEN	02468	SHELL
M.F. HALL	02482	SHELL
D.J. JAKEMAN	02410	SHELL
R.H. SCOTT	02453	SHELL
R.E. WEGMAN	02454	SHELL
D.V. DAVIS AND WIFE	01490	BP
J. BROWNLOW	00485	D/H IR.
R. DYKSTRA	00231	D/H D
W.L. JENSEN	00110	D/H A
A.LUBIENSKI	00126	D/H B
J.R. SLOCUM	05069	TEXACO
H.J. TIGHE	00347	D/H B
G.K. O'BRIEN	00556	D/H C
S. KRUEGER	00576	D/H A
B. MUNRO	00577	D/H C

ABADAN

E. OBIKEN	00659	D/H G
G.D. BLYTHE	00434	D/H C
G.A. CAMERON	04128	SOCAL
T.J. COLLINGS	00881	D/H B
M.M. CRANE	00878	D/H A
D. ELLIOTT	00587	D/H C

(CONTINUED)

PAGE THREE GP1

G GROTHEER	00810	IRICON
A. FLEMING	00680	D/H V
T.J. GORMAN	09809	IRICON
P.E. KIRSCHKE	00380	D/H A
M.G. HASSON	00390	D/H B
J.F.P. MURPHY	00613	D/H C
K. PLESNER	00328	D/H DAN.
A.F. TEAL	02477	SHELL

FIELDS

J.R. ALLMARK AND WIFE	00186	D/H B
R.J. KADALA	03215	EXXON
D.C. BARRELLE	00653	D/H A
F.A. COSTELLO	GPPYEW	D/H B

TEHERAN

W.C. BELLENGER AND WIFE	04150	SOCAL
J.H. VOSS	00599	D/H G

THE FOLLOWING NEED CLARIFICATION FROM YOUR LIST
AHWAZ
DSON
J. HAGE (EX MECON)
M. HARDING (QUERY NIOC)

ABADAN
WILLIAMS (PLEASE GIVE INITIALS

TEHERAN
G. CLARKE (COULD THIS BE R.A. CLARK 00224 OR G.J. CLARKE 00709
OR T.G. CLARKE 00832)

ENDS
MR PORTER 2
MR BAYMAN 2
MR GLOSS 2
NORMAL CIRC
SENT 1100/2 BH

Appendix 13

Outward Message | ACTION: | CC: /

FROM IROS LDN GMX
TO OILSERVCO AHWAZ

FOR EVANS FROM PORTER

GP C16   04.01.79
FURTHER TO MY GP C15 (EYES ALONE)

LAWSON SPOKE TO ME FROM BAHREIN AND INDICATED THERE MIGHT STILL
BE A NUMBER OF CONTRACTOR RELATED PERSONNEL TO BE MOVED OUT AND
THAT YOU MIGHT WISH TO RECONSIDER DECISIONS TO CANCEL 737
ORIGINALLY SCHEDULED FOR TODAY. UNDERSTAND IT IS JUST POSSIBLE
THAT WE COULD ARRANGE FOR IT TO BE REINSTATED IF YOU SO WISH.
THIS WOULD NOT AFFECT THE 737 FLIGHT ALREADY BOOKED FOR SUNDAY
7TH JANUARY.
WOULD YOU PLEASE ADVISE ME.

REGARDS PORTER
...
GS

RCD VIA PHONE MR PORTER 0725GMT
SENT AHWAZ 073XGMT
DIST:
MR PORTER 2

MR BAYMAN 4

MR GLOSS 2 (NORMAL CIRC:)

Lightning Source UK Ltd.
Milton Keynes UK
21 September 2010

160157UK00001B/30/P